WORKING
ACTOR

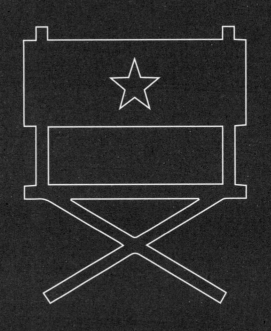

WORKING
ACTOR

Breaking In, Making a Living,
and Making a Life in the Fabulous
Trenches of Show Business

DAVID DEAN BOTTRELL

TEN SPEED PRESS
California | New York

Published in the United States by Ten Speed Press, an imprint of the Crown Publishing
Group, a division of Penguin Random House LLC, New York.
www.crownpublishing.com
www.tenspeed.com

Ten Speed Press and the Ten Speed Press colophon are registered trademarks of
Penguin Random House LLC.

Library of Congress Cataloging-in-Publication Data is on file with the publisher.

Trade Paperback ISBN: 978-0-399-58190-8
eBook ISBN: 978-0-399-58191-5

Printed in the United States of America

Design by Michelle Li

10 9 8 7 6 5 4 3 2 1

First Edition

*For Edward Bates, David E. Kelley,
Nikki Valko, and Nick Wilkinson,
without whom I would never have
worked a day in this business.*

CONTENTS

part three | **Keeping the Door Open**

**THE BEST THING ABOUT
SHOW BUSINESS?**
I love when we all collaborate together
to create something beautiful.

—Sarah, recent drama school grad

**THE WORST THING ABOUT
SHOW BUSINESS?**
Explaining it to other people.

—Taz, recent drama school grad

INTRODUCTION

Why I Wrote This Book

A few years ago, I put together a few of my funnier spoken word stories and created a comedic solo show about my tumultuous love life entitled *David Dean Bottrell Makes Love: A One-Man Show*. Much to my surprise, it proved to be a big underground hit and played for eighteen months in L.A. A couple of months into the run, the *Los Angeles Times* showed up and gave the show a very kind review. Needless to say, I was thrilled, but there was one comment that really bugged me. In the paragraph that introduced me to their readers, who'd perhaps never heard of me, I was referred to as "an L.A. actor-comedian-writer on the fringe of success."

"The fringe of success"? Were they freaking kidding?

I had (for the most part) supported myself as a working professional in the entertainment industry—the world's toughest industry to make a living in—for over thirty years. Yet apparently I was only on the "fringe" of success? Okay, granted, I was living in Los Angeles, a city utterly convinced that the only definition of a successful performer is a famous performer, but this unasked-for career assessment weirdly stung me to my core.

It got me thinking about what "success" in show business looks like. I suppose that, like a lot of artists, I'd been existing in that perpetual state of waiting; doing job after job while holding onto the idea that one of these days a very special, very particular gig would show up that would be the game changer, the job that would firmly plant me on the magical list of people who could expect to keep working consistently until they died. Of course, I knew that no such list actually exists, but show business is an industry fueled by far-reaching and seductive dreams.

That's when I asked myself the big question: Had my dream already come true? Was I already living it?

Since I began this journey (over three decades ago), I've been fortunate to land enough writing and acting gigs to pay my bills, contribute to my retirement account, and take a modest vacation each year. In short, I've clawed my way to the middle. By most people's standards, I guess that makes me a success. Like many of my peers, I leaped into the entertainment industry early in life without the slightest idea of what I was getting into. Having been at this for a while now, I actually know a few very famous and successful people. Because I also teach and mentor, each year I meet and work with a talented crop of hopeful newcomers, all champing at the bit for their shot at the big time. I consider myself lucky. My career choice has, for the most part, worked out well—but not without a few hard-learned lessons along the way. I am now (in the grand pecking order of show business) considered a veteran. And like most vets, I have a few war stories to tell.

So, after a fair amount of nail-biting, I decided to write this book about what to expect if you are contemplating a career in show business. Here on these tear-stained, blood-spattered pages, I'll try to share the bigger lessons I have learned, along with a few things to avoid if possible. This is a book about making a living (and making a life) while trying to pursue a very particular dream.

I happen to love show business. Even with all its ups and downs, it still strikes me as a swell way to spend one's life. If you approach the industry with a clear vision—to make your living creatively—I happen to believe it's an achievable goal. As you will see in the upcoming pages, I'm probably one of the least-qualified candidates imaginable, but somehow, I did it—and continue to do it. Assuming you have talent and a lot of determination, and you genuinely enjoy challenges, you can too.

By the Way . . .

I didn't want my voice to be the only one heard from in this book, so I invited some friends of mine to contribute a few thoughts about their lives and careers as well. Since I wanted everyone to speak with complete candor, I assured them that their real names would not be used. You'll notice that not all of them are performers. There's a reason for that. Actors do not work in a vacuum. Your career will be spent in constant interaction with writers, directors, producers, agents, managers, casting directors, and so on, so it's good to start getting to know them a bit. Among the individuals quoted, pretty much every race, sexual preference, and major religion is represented. Some are immigrants. Some are transgender. Some are artists with disabilities. Some are hugely successful. Some are middle class. And some are just beginning their careers. They range in age from nineteen to eighty-four. I thank them all for their wonderfully generous, hilarious, and honest contributions to this book.

I ASKED A FEW OF MY WISE, WONDERFUL FRIENDS: WHAT'S THE BEST/WORST THING ABOUT SHOW BUSINESS?

BEST THING?

Through the characters we portray, we can show an audience that it's okay to make mistakes. Mistakes make life far more interesting.

WORST THING?

Like in any other job, some people are assholes.

—Nathan, up-and-coming young actor and recent drama school grad

BEST THING?

The "show" part.

WORST THING?

The phone calls.

—Andrew, TV writer, series creator, and showrunner

BEST THING?

The landscape of your life keeps changing. You never know where you will be working or who you will be working with. You can go from a play to a movie to a television show. You may sign a contract for a week or a year. You may wear your own clothes or be at a fashion house being fitted with the most divine couture clothes. The uncertainty of what's around the corner makes life interesting and exciting.

WORST THING?

The landscape of your life keeps changing. Uncertainty about where your next job is coming from is unsettling. Inevitably, you will buy tickets for that long-anticipated trip—and you will get a job. You will commit to being a bridesmaid at your friend's wedding—and the part of a lifetime comes along. So you cannot make plans; you cannot really budget your time or money, because what's ahead is a mystery.

—Roz, popular theatre, TV, and film actor

PART ONE

FINDING THE DOOR

Some people leap into pursuing their dreams
with little to no preparation.

Sometimes this works out fine. I'm living proof of that.

That said, if I had it all to do over again, I'd have
approached a few things differently.

**THE BEST THING ABOUT
SHOW BUSINESS?**
You wake up every morning
full of hope and optimism.

**THE WORST THING ABOUT
SHOW BUSINESS?**
You go to bed each night full
of despair.

—Mike, actor and writer

1

THE BIG QUESTION

———

Should I Do This with My Life?

A few years ago, I started teaching a couple of acting classes. It's been fun to be surrounded by so many talented young people, all with a real desire to learn and get better at their craft. Recently, one of my students took me aside and nervously asked if I thought she had the talent to "make it." The question took me by surprise. Mostly because she's quite good. I was happy to reassure her that it was certainly possible that she could make it, provided the gods of show business smiled in her direction.

The conversation flashed me back to when I was a twenty-year-old wannabe actor living in Austin, Texas, and desperately wondering if I had the goods to "make it" in New York. I was terrified of failing, but also feared the possibility of going to my grave wishing I'd at least tried. I had, at the time, a truly horrible job. I think this job doesn't even exist today. I was a file clerk. Five days a week, I worked in the basement of a large insurance company, where I literally filed files all day long. Lit by fluorescent tubes, "the tomb" (as those of us who worked there called it) was a long, windowless room, lined floor to ceiling with tall racks of insurance files. From 8:00 a.m. to 5:00 p.m., I climbed up and down a rolling ladder, pulling the lists of requested files and then refiling the files I had pulled the day before. It was grim, mind-numbing, soulless work. And it was the perfect job for me.

The utter boredom allowed me to daydream pretty much nonstop. I knew I wanted to be an artist. I knew I wanted to make something of myself. Yet I also knew I could be totally comfortable staying in Austin. The city was (and still is) a virtual Eden for regional artists. There was always plenty to do and see and hear. Yet part of me desperately wanted to measure myself against the big-timers in New York. Austin could never offer stardom. They didn't give Oscars, Emmys, or Tonys for Best File Clerk.

At the time, I was also appearing in a play at one of the local community theatres. It was a British drawing room comedy, one of those old chestnuts you could bring your grandmother to without being worried that someone would say the F word or take off their clothes. One night, I arrived at the theatre completely exhausted after eight hours of nonstop filing. I was cranky and depressed and felt (at age twenty) that my life was already over. Who was I? Just another penniless college dropout with no game plan.

I pulled on my costume and trudged out to the wings. As I listened to the audience filing in, I started thinking about the glamorous Westgate Dinner Theatre on the opposite side of town. It was an Equity house that booked professional touring shows. I knew that at this very moment, those actors were also standing in the wings waiting for their performance to start; the difference was, they were getting paid! Were they more talented? Were they more driven? Did they have "connections"? I knew that dinner theatre wasn't exactly the big time, but it looked pretty damn good from where I was standing at the moment.

As the houselights went down, I tugged at my uncomfortable collar. Who was I kidding? Our little amateur production now seemed shabby and embarrassing. My back hurt from climbing a ladder all day. I had paper cuts on nine of my fingers. All I wanted was to get this over with and go home. Hearing my cue, I sighed and marched dutifully out on stage. And that's when it happened.

The play was being staged in the round with audience on all four sides. Unlike a normal proscenium stage—where the lights are in your eyes—when you walked out onto this stage, you were keenly aware of the audience. I don't know why, but on this particular night, I noticed them in a way I hadn't before. As I hit the edge of the playing area, the whole audience turned their faces toward me—and smiled! This group of total strangers seemed oddly happy to see me, and I hadn't even done anything yet! The very fact that I was even willing to put on this funny costume and at least try to entertain them had won me a totally unearned place in their hearts. It was like a tsunami of goodwill had just washed over me. All of a sudden, I wasn't tired anymore. A bolt of energy shot through my body, and I dove into delivering the best comic performance I could muster.

The rest of the evening seemed magical. The cast landed every joke, every sight gag. The applause went on longer than usual, and we managed to steal an extra bow in our goofy period costumes. A few people even waited in the lobby to shake our hands. That night, as I steered my dented Buick out of the parking lot, I knew that if there was even a ghost of a chance I might be able to do this for a living, I had to pursue it. I was going to New York to be an actor.

Seven months later (on a song and a prayer), I did.

Of course, my hope was that my talent and charm would be recognized quickly and rewarded in short order with major stardom. That's not exactly how it worked out. In fact, I'm still waiting for that to happen. The transition from amateur to professional was neither as easy nor as hard as I'd expected. It began with a healthy dose of humility, followed by a few years of extreme poverty, interlaced with quite a bit of incredibly hard work. I'm not sure exactly how I fueled my ambition during that stretch, but I do know that I steadfastly harbored an unshakable faith that this dream I was chasing was the most wonderful destiny a young man could ever wish for. I guess it worked. I'm still here.

If you are contemplating taking the plunge, don't expect your family and friends to cheer when you announce that you're dropping out of college or giving up a perfectly good career in accounting to chase after some impossible dream. Given the odds, your loved ones would be remiss if they didn't ask, "Why attempt this?"

The answer is surprisingly simple: When it works, it's heaven.

When the pieces come together, and you experience that rush of artist, material, and audience all meeting in some sort of harmonic convergence, the feeling is indescribable. It's like having an orgasm, while eating a hot fudge sundae, while lying on a huge pile of cash that you just won in the lottery, that just happens to be heaped on the grave of that kid who beat you up in elementary school. It's heaven. Heaven on earth.

The word "amateur" comes to us from the Latin *amator*, meaning "lover," from *amare*, which means "to love." To love, when you are young and relatively inno-cent, is, of course, quite easy. You are filled with nothing but great expectations and very little real experience to temper those dreams. Grown-up love (the kind that lasts, anyway) involves loving not just the dream, but also the reality. I try to instill in my students that most careers are a wonderful mashup of the good, the bad, and the ugly. Glorious victories. Crappy disappointments. Rapturous praise. Rotten tomatoes. Enduring friendships. Freaks and fiends. Lavish attention followed by stretches of complete and utter invisibility. So how does a sane person justify this? They don't. Sane people don't enter this business. They wouldn't be happy here. They don't understand.

To be an artist, you have to be a dreamer. But when I say dreamer, I don't mean couch potato. Show business is a competitive sport that attracts some very skilled and intimidating players. It takes a certain kind of person to willingly suit up in your best gear and take to the field, knowing full well that you are going to get clobbered a few times before you ever get anywhere near the goal line. If that doesn't scare you too much, this might be the job for you—which brings us back to our original question.

Should you do this with your life? You tell me. Chances are if you have purchased this book, the affair has already begun. And who am I to stand in the way of love?

Congratulations. Welcome to show business.

Seven things you might want to consider before launching:

1. If you can be happy doing anything else with your life, do it. I'm not saying show business isn't fun, rewarding, and sometimes very profitable, but it is a huge gamble. And you will be gambling with some of the most important years of your life. If you're not the gambling type, don't do it. Live in the real world instead. It's actually a terrific place once you get used to it.

2. Show business is conducted in major cities. That means you'll have to move to one of them. If you're looking to play in the big leagues, that means New York or L.A. Both cities are expensive. There are some other smaller but equally viable markets, so look before you leap. Moving to a new place is expensive, so bring as much money as you can scrape together. I'm not kidding.

3. If you are young and want to be a creative artist, don't go to "regular" college to study your craft. If you want to go to college, that's great! But unless it's one of the really hot ones (like Yale, NYU, Juilliard, USC, UCLA), you'll probably just have to start over once you're out of school. My suggestion: If you want to go to college far from the major capitals of entertainment, then don't study acting there. Study something practical that might help you earn a living or that will enrich you as a person. If you want to study your craft, do it in the city where you intend to pursue it. And do it in the best school or studio that city has to offer (which might not be an accredited university). If you really want to learn how to swim, get in the deep end of the pool with the other ambitious kids and start splashing.

4. You'll need to support yourself. That means you'll need to go out and find a crappy job. You'll also need a cheap place to live and at least one reasonably sane roommate. This period of your life can actually be a lot of fun (especially when you are young). You will have some adventures and will probably make some wonderful, hilarious lifelong friends.

5. A very small percentage of people make money right out of the gate in show business. Most people's careers don't come together until they are in their thirties (or later). If you already know that you'll need a large and steady supply of money in order to be happy, you might want to consider another profession, like bank robbery.

6. Have fun, but keep focused. You're here to do something. So do it. Don't fart around. Time is valuable. Start testing yourself. Find out if you like doing this.

7. Enjoy yourself! More on that later.

I'm in New York because the work is honored here, and craft comes before looks, youth, and bucks.

—Rachel, stage and TV actor

2

THEY SAY THE NEON LIGHTS ARE BRIGHT

———

Starting in New York

When I was eighteen, I left my family's home and flew to Austin, Texas, to start my freshman year as a theatre major at St. Edward's University. The school's small theatre department boasted an auditorium modeled after Washington's prestigious Arena Stage and had a unique program that brought in veteran Broadway actors like Eileen Heckart and George Grizzard to appear in plays with the students—thus giving them a unique chance to learn from the real pros. I knew who Ms. Heckart and Mr. Grizzard were because I had seen their faces many times while poring obsessively over the "Best Plays" yearbooks in my local library. As a young theatre geek, I could not have been more excited!

Unfortunately, when I arrived in Austin, I discovered that the theatre department had changed direction and now was being led by a guy whose background was primarily in dinner theatre. Consequently, the "guest artists" being brought down to perform were largely people who'd once had a little fame in TV or the movies but were now desperately in search of a paycheck. Any paycheck. Many of them were battle-scarred, embittered old alcoholics with not a lot to say to the students other than "get out of my light" or "always stand behind me."

After finishing my freshman year, I decided to leave St. Edward's. I was tired of dealing with old drunks who didn't know their lines and occasionally tried to jam their hand down your pants (more later about dealing with bad behavior). Although

I didn't learn much about acting that year, I did learn quite a bit about show business. Mostly, I learned that I didn't want to end up like any of these actors that I'd come to refer to as "guest losers." As I mentioned earlier, I hung around Austin for two more years, mostly working pointless jobs and appearing in the local theatre productions with wonderfully funny people. To this day I wonder if I should have stayed there, but I wanted to know more. I wanted to know if I could make it.

New York seemed like the only answer. Prior to moving there, I'd spent exactly one afternoon in the city and had no idea what I was getting myself into. I attended a regional audition for NYU and was accepted. I had no money to pay for it, but I decided to worry about that later. I scraped together a few bucks and bought myself a bus ticket to New York City. Before leaving Austin, I cleverly managed to sublet an apartment in Manhattan from a guy who was going to school at the University of Texas. I had heard through the grapevine that you were always supposed to ask where the apartment was. I knew neighborhoods and geography mattered, but that was about all I knew. When I asked him the apartment's location, he smiled slyly and said, "It's on Broadway." My heart skipped a beat! Broadway! That's where I was going anyway! How convenient. I'd be close to work! I forked over $200 in cash, and he promised I'd be met at the bus station by a guy wearing a hat, named DeAngelo, who would hand me the keys.

After two days on the bus, I arrived at Port Authority at 2:00 a.m. on a Saturday morning. Port Authority was, at the time, dirty and intimidating, and the clientele who frequented the place at that time of night were not super friendly-looking. Greyhound had managed to lose all my luggage, so all I had was the clothes on my back and a backpack containing my journal, a toothbrush, and a couple of worn paperbacks. Wearing my naiveté like a badge of honor, I bravely marched up to every guy in a hat I could find at 2:00 a.m. in Port Authority and asked if his name was DeAngelo, and amazingly, I eventually found him. He turned out to be very nice and quickly assessed that I was a total rube. He handed me the keys and carefully explained to me how to get to my new apartment. Ten minutes later, I boarded my first ever subway.

At 4:00 a.m., I discovered that the description "on Broadway" turned out to be Broadway at 141st Street in West Harlem, which at that time was a very rugged neighborhood with some serious drug problems. As it turned out, I didn't need a key, since the previous tenants had taken the door lock with them when they left. The building was a rundown disaster with no heat or hot water. The unit had no phone, so there was no option to call for help. And (as I would later learn) I had arrived on the coldest day of that particular winter. On my first night in New York, I slept sitting up with my back against my unlocked door, afraid that if I lay down, I would freeze to death.

Fortunately, I had two friends (acquaintances really) who had recently moved to New York from Austin, and they graciously helped me get through the five long weeks I lived in that scary apartment. Finally, I managed to escape to a slightly less dangerous neighborhood known as Alphabet City, a little east of the East Village. Then, on my one-year anniversary of moving to New York, I finally moved into a modest but safe apartment on a decent block in midtown.

More than once during that first year, I wondered if New York was going to kill me (and I don't mean that in the figurative sense). To this day, I'm amazed that I survived. New York is a city, with a capital C, and I pretty much had straw sticking out of my hair when I first arrived. Fortunately, I was (and still am) a fast learner and by nature optimistic. Even during my first night in that horrid apartment, I remember thinking, *It will never get any worse than this. It will only get better.* And it did.

In those days, New York was pretty much an entirely theatrical community. There was very little TV production, and only a few films were being shot there. As I write this book, that has shifted tremendously, with a great many TV shows currently making their home in Manhattan. Films also have rediscovered the city. To compete with the country's other "live entertainment capital," Las Vegas, much of Broadway has embraced a "more is more" commercial aesthetic, which sort of makes sense given that the majority of the audience members are now tourists. But there's still some art going on there as well.

For an actor, theatre is one of the most rigorous professions imaginable. To be successful in that market means being able to knock out eight shows a week without collapsing. And the quality of your work must be pretty much top drawer. You must have the mental and physical stamina to make yourself heard and seen and understood in the back row of the balcony, and you must love to work for the ticket-buyers. Audiences are an active and hugely important character in the theatre. You are guiding the audience through the experience, and it must always be fresh. You can't give Tuesday's performance on Wednesday. If you are a musical performer, you need to be able to do *all* of the above *and* sing and dance incredibly well. And did I mention the part about eight shows a week?

If you're a playwright or director, the standards are even higher, for the simple reason that there are even fewer jobs. Although every play or musical might employ a fair number of actors, it will have only one director and one writer (or a team of writers if it's a musical). The vast majority of theatre productions live or die based on the reviews. As you might have heard, the critics in New York are not known for being terribly kind to shows that fall short of their somewhat high expectations.

You can make a nice living as a theatre artist if you are fortunate enough to work in large Broadway venues (with 500-plus seats); or you can make a somewhat more modest living in the smaller off-Broadway houses (499 seats or less). New York's prestigious nonprofit theatre world doesn't offer large paychecks either, but it does offer the best material. Many careers are made in these venues where brave producers can take much bigger risks and present challenging or more stylized material. It can be a very exciting place to work.

For those wanting to work in TV and films, there are now production studios open around the city churning out everything from crime drama to three-camera sitcoms. The city also still offers income opportunities to performers via commercials, voice-overs, and industrial films that can offer a decent paycheck and take very little time to shoot.

New York has a notoriously hectic pace and a wildly diverse population. It is also a city where you can comfortably live with no car—provided you're okay with walking, stairs, subways, buses, and bikes, or can afford rideshares or cabs. It is densely populated, and New Yorkers coexist shoulder-to-shoulder. It is not a particularly quiet place, although it still has a few peaceful pockets here and there. It also, of course, has some of the finest music, dance, theatre, and art in the world. It's the home of the Yankees, Wall Street, and astonishing architecture. All forms of performance are in abundance all around, including surprisingly great street performers singing, playing, and dancing for donations in the subway.

In short, to be an artist in New York is to play with the big kids. Quality is the name of the game. To succeed here means putting yourself up against the best of the best. This city reveres the imagination and triumphs of the creative mind. If you're an artist who loves to solve complex puzzles or find the newest, most mind-bending expression of a timeless idea; if you love history, culture, justice, art, architecture, and staying up late and arguing with people about religion, philosophy, art, and politics, New York might be the city for you. God knows it's produced many, many world-class artists and continues to do so. There are other cities that can provide a similarly colorful environment—Chicago and San Francisco come to mind—but none has the electricity of New York.

Be aware that New York is a tough market and thrives on honesty. If it doesn't love you, it will let you know in no uncertain terms. That is not to say that if you don't connect with New York, you suck. It could be that you're just in the wrong city. Maybe L.A. is more your speed. And we'll talk about that next.

If you're considering New York, scope it out—and consider the cost. New York has become incredibly expensive. It seriously ain't cheap. If you want to enter this market, you'll not only need to live here, you'll also need enough money for classes, headshots, and other expenses you never imagined. Actors in New York are often bartenders, waiters, nannies, tutors, delivery people, office temps, you name it. I have a friend who has always loved playing bridge and has turned teaching the game and playing in tournaments into a viable way to make a living.

If you are meant to start here, you'll know it. You'll find a way to make the money you need. Every newcomer faces the challenge of finding a gig that will pay the bills. There are no real rules to this other than that you need to be clever enough to manage your money gigs so they allow time for your professional obligations (auditions, rehearsals, classes). It can be done. There are many people doing it even as you read this.

New York is its own universe. It can inspire you and it can wear you down. Not everybody stays here forever. But if you can carve out a place for yourself here (even for a while), it will teach you a great deal about yourself, and you can be proud of that achievement for the rest of your life.

Five things to keep in mind before moving to New York:

1. It is a very crowded urban wonderland, and everyone lives very close together.

2. It costs a lot to live here. There are still a few areas where the housing is considered "affordable," but even those areas will seem expensive if you're coming from a smaller place.

3. New York has a winter. It also has a spring, summer, and fall.

4. If you want to work in theatre, New York represents the pinnacle. It's where the standard for stage performers is the highest.

5. New York is currently enjoying a wave of TV and film production. Desirable roles in both media are now regularly cast here.

I ASKED A FEW OF MY EAST COAST FRIENDS: WHY ARE YOU BASED IN NEW YORK?

New York keeps the onus on the work. L.A. feels like a one-industry town. New York, because of its diversity, is more interesting.
—Zachary, TV, film, and stage actor

New York always has more appealing movies shooting here than in L.A.
—Parker, TV and film actor

New York is primarily a theatre town. For the most part, shows are first developed here. I like to be in on the ground level. Also, my family is nearby.
—Claire, musical theatre and TV actor

California has blown it when it comes to keeping the industry in L.A. With all this production happening, New York is thriving. We've got about sixty TV series here! And movies!
—Susanne, TV and indie film director

New York is tougher than L.A., but it makes you stronger. It's where art matters.
—Aaron, TV and theatre director

I am based in New York because I like to take a walk at times and not be looked at like the aliens that walked off the ship in *Close Encounters of the Third Kind.* And I like to eat after the sun goes down and not before.
—Kyle, TV and film actor and director

I love the city. It's real, it's authentic.
—Talia, TV and film character actor

After starting my career in L.A., New York seemed like more of a long-term option, a place where aging wasn't as detrimental and where theatre was supported. It was also an opportunity to start over (which is both good and bad) and hit the "reset" button. And there was a guy here.

—Gabrielle, actor, comedian, and sketch performer

I feel more myself on the East Coast, which means I write better here.

—Simon, playwright and TV writer

I live in New York because I hate the phrase "No worries." Everyone in L.A., all the time: "No worries, no worries!" And I'm just like, "Um . . . I actually have a lot of worries." I also (as a single guy) appreciate that on the East Coast I'm at least a full point hotter than I am on the West Coast, and that not everyone I talk to is involved in entertainment, so it's not all a giant circular firing squad.

—Ari, TV writer, playwright, and producer

You can live a pretty great existence in L.A. even while being poor.

—Mike, L.A.-based actor and writer

3

WELCOME TO THE HOTEL CALIFORNIA

———

Starting in Los Angeles

The first time I came to California, it was to visit a former roommate of mine who had decided that L.A. might be a better fit for her. At the time, I considered myself a dedicated New York actor with no plans to leave. I'd just worked for a fairly prestigious theatre and had gotten a nice write-up in the *New York Times*. This had utterly convinced me that my future lay in forging a career onstage (with maybe an occasional Oscar-winning film role thrown in).

The morning I boarded the plane at JFK, it was horribly cold, with a wind chill factor somewhere around "sudden death." When I arrived at LAX, still wearing my parka, I spotted my former roommate waiting for me, wearing a black leather miniskirt. We screamed and kissed and ran out into the gorgeous California night. It was about 10:00 p.m., and the weather was incredibly balmy and warm. Peeling off my parka, I tossed it and my duffle bag into the backseat of her vintage, mint condition 1966 convertible Fiat, and we sped off into the L.A. night with the top down. I remember staring up at the rows of palm trees flying by overhead and screaming, "This is freaking paradise!"

Within a few minutes, we were exiting the freeway and speeding around some hair-pin turns on what I would soon learn was Laurel Canyon Boulevard. Suddenly, we cut a hard left and began to climb higher and higher on steep, narrow roads until we reached what appeared to me to be the very top of the canyon. We stopped at what (at night, anyway) seemed like a fairly ordinary-looking house—that is, until we started descending some scary-looking wooden stairs on the side, finally reaching a metal screen door that led to her apartment.

It was the coolest space I'd ever seen. Her two-story unit hung cantilevered over the side of a cliff. Its huge glass windows looked out from the very top of Laurel Canyon across to the opposite side (a towering hilltop named, appropriately enough, Mount Olympus). We stepped out onto the balcony, and we seemed to be magically suspended in midair. From this gorgeous vantage point, you couldn't even see the city—just the twinkling lights of Mt. Olympus far across the canyon. This high up, you could barely hear the rolling traffic on the curvy canyon road far, far below. The breeze was cool. And the moon was full.

I couldn't believe how gorgeous this place was. I looked over at my friend. "This is freaking paradise," I said again. The words seemed lame, but it was the best I could do. My friend nodded. I was exhausted, but my friend had invited "a few friends" over, and within an hour the house was rocking to the point where it felt like it might shake loose from the side of the canyon. Everyone was young, gorgeous, hilarious, filled with energy, and loaded with ambition. None of these people were from New York. They were from everywhere from Toledo to Timbuktu, all here to spin the wheel in Hollywood. It was an incredibly fun night. It felt like a celebration. I wasn't sure what of, but it was definitely a celebration of something, and I didn't want to miss it.

I woke the next morning in the spare bedroom, still in the clothes I'd boarded the plane in. I knew it was morning by the clear, gently filtered light slipping in from behind the window shade. I tiptoed out to the kitchen and made myself some coffee. Slowly, I made my way down to the living room. As I carefully stepped between a couple of the guests, who had either camped out or lost consciousness on the carpet, I was drawn to the balcony by the most amazing sight I'd ever seen.

The entire canyon was filled with a ginormous bank of beautiful white fog. I literally couldn't see a thing. It looked like our little canyon house had somehow floated up into heaven, effortlessly levitating miles above the magical city below.

Stepping out onto the balcony, I couldn't believe how peaceful and enchanted it felt. I pulled a slightly damp director's chair over to the balcony rail and carefully climbed into it. My head was still throbbing from the multiple vodka tonics I'd knocked back the night before, but I couldn't believe what I was witnessing. "This is freaking paradise," I heard myself whisper.

Then I heard a sound. At first, I didn't recognize it. It was rhythmic and steady and was coming toward me through the fog. As the sound drew closer, I began to feel scared. Like I should run or duck. Then suddenly out of the cloud bank emerged a huge hawk. It was coming straight at me until suddenly its wings straightened and stiffened. Its body tilted and arced into a huge, seemingly effortless circle. After soaring within a few feet of me, it silently disappeared into the fog again. My mouth fell open.

"Holy crap!"

For the next week, I was introduced to the amusement park that was L.A. Hikes in the mountains, the Pacific Ocean, the nightspots, the food, the music scene, and most of all, the sunshine—the endless, bright, warming sunshine—in December! It was the most fun place I'd ever been. My friend was very good at making friends, and she seemed to know a lot of people who were experiencing some very big success in the entertainment business, and they had the houses to prove it. Huge, beautiful places with big green yards filled with palm trees, cacti, and exotic flowers. L.A. seemed like a garden that grew beautiful people, beautiful dreams, and big, beautiful piles of money.

I knew I had to come back and give it a try. If these other actors could do it, so could I. So I did. And it was a disaster.

Unlike my beautiful friend, I did not land in a gorgeous house on top of Laurel Canyon, but lived in a series of crappy sublets and stressful roommate situations ranging from the San Fernando Valley to Silver Lake to some of the less appealing sections of Hollywood. I was driving not a sexy convertible Fiat, but an aging Chevrolet that tended to break down in traffic every other day. No sooner had I arrived than the agent who was supposed to rep me backed out of the agreement. The sun wasn't warm—it was hot. And it shone down on me and my rotten life every damn day. It was relentless and interminable. I hated it.

After six months, I packed my bags and returned to New York. Two years later, I returned to L.A., but this time as a writer (with an off-Broadway play behind me). Although my new L.A. career also got off to a rocky start, a path emerged for me, and eventually I had a lengthy and lucrative run, writing screenplays for Hollywood studios. My boyfriend and I found a nice place to live. It wasn't on top of a canyon, but it was very nice. I learned to like California. And in return, California started liking me.

My original intent was to stay for three to six months. I stayed for twenty-two years.

I can honestly say that I have nothing but great affection for Los Angeles, but unlike New York, which is a city, L.A. is a place. It's actually a whole bunch of places that all sort of grew into each other, and collectively they all make up a very big, very nice place. L.A. is the epicenter of the entertainment industry. Pretty much all the big stuff emanates from there, and if fortune smiles on you in the TV and film business, you can do very, very well. The aesthetic of Hollywood sort of hangs over the city, and depending on where you live and the circles you run in, L.A. can feel like a total company town. Or not.

If you like being outside, it's hard to beat it, since the sun shines most of the time. Not much happens in the way of weather, but when it does, it's usually biblical. Nature doesn't screw around in SoCal. Sometimes it rains so hard that people's houses slide off hillsides. The Santa Ana winds can take down trees. Sometimes the whole place utterly dries out and the outlying areas are threatened by huge, dangerous fires. And every once in a while there's a big, scary earthquake like the one I experienced on January 17, 1994, at 4:30 a.m., when I scrambled out of bed, lodged myself in a door frame, and watched as the pictures were shaken off the walls.

L.A. is a car town, and it's very challenging to navigate the city without one. On the plus side, you can drive two hours in any direction on the many freeways and be in a totally different environment—the desert, the forests, the mountains (or you can arrive in a different country if you drive really fast). On the downside, you can also spend two hours stuck in traffic and travel only about thirty blocks.

There are far too many people. Way too many cars. The city offers all kinds of culture, but mostly people don't go to see it. It has a lot to do with traffic and also with the vibe of the city. People love their homes in L.A. I suppose it has to do with how long it takes to "get home," so once they get there they like to stay home and watch movies or TV shows on Netflix. Although there is a lively local theatre scene, it is mostly actors acting in small venues for an audience of fellow actors. So it's fun, but strange at the same time. The larger professional theatres (as is true in many other cities) are scrambling for an audience, and that audience seems to get older each year. The improv, stand-up, music, and sketch comedy scenes are huge. Some of the best film schools are here. If you want to write for TV, it would be dumb to live anywhere else. L.A. also has an astoundingly gorgeous population—I suspect this is because for the last hundred years the most beautiful people on the planet have been moving here to get into the movie business. And they're still coming. The best parties I have ever attended in my life happened in L.A.

Success in Los Angeles is not always skill-based. Sometimes it is truly luck-based, and that's as frustrating as it is wonderful. In that sense, it's a truly democratic town. Success is gauged not by your classical theatre training but by your appeal. So if you're gorgeous or sexy or super edgy or utterly hilarious and that is deemed something America or the world might like, a lot of doors can open pretty fast.

It's also a city with a very short memory. A surprising number of people who had really successful runs oddly fall out of fashion and are quickly deemed irrelevant. You'd be surprised who you'll run into at the car wash. I've been "nobody" in L.A. and I've been the flavor of the month. I once had a writing job, in which I didn't have to do much actual writing, that paid me $10,000 a week to attend meetings. I had a lot of fun in L.A., and for many people it's the Garden of Eden. For me, living there felt like I was on some kind of permanent vacation.

It has also become incredibly expensive. Brace yourself.

If you're the kind of artist who likes to quickly pull together a new scene and then knock it out on the Paramount lot at 7:00 a.m., this is your town. If you like cars, travel, surfing, horses, movies, gardening, the great outdoors, skiing, hiking in the canyons or mountains, working out at the gym, alternative medicine, and dating some of the most beautiful people imaginable, L.A. might be the perfect place to build your career. On the downside, if you are not a self-starter or a person who likes driving or being proactive on the social circuit, L.A. can be a little isolating. That said, it is a huge piece of real estate, and there are many opportunities to define and redefine yourself as an artist. The pace is relaxed. The city is patient. And despite the air quality (which is not great), you can breathe here.

Five things to keep in mind before moving to Los Angeles:

1. L.A. is a very crowded place that doesn't seem so crowded because it's spread out over such a huge area. The only time it will seem crowded is when you try to get somewhere in your car in less than an hour. It is almost impossible to live in L.A. without a car.

2. It is also very expensive. The housing is more plentiful, comfortable, and larger than New York's, but be prepared for sticker shock when you see the prices.

3. L.A. does not have a winter. It only has spring, summer, and fall (and they all sort of blend together). There's a rainy season from late fall to early spring that is not always all that rainy. When the area does experience a mild rain, the local news coverage will make it sound like the city has been hit by a monsoon.

4. If you want to work exclusively in TV and film, L.A. is the center of that universe. The West Coast branch of the industry is interested in people and products with mass appeal. Here, show business is definitely a *business*, so brace yourself.

5. L.A. does have theatre (some of it quite good), but productions struggle to find an audience, since going to plays is not so much a part of the cultural life of this particular city.

I ASKED A FEW OF MY WEST COAST FRIENDS: WHY ARE YOU BASED IN L.A.?

The majority of TV and film work is in L.A.
—Ivan, well-known comic actor, writer, and producer

The weather.
—Danielle, film and television producer and network executive

Because I want to work in movies and I hate cold weather.
—Nathan, up-and-coming young actor and recent drama school grad

It's easier to raise a family in L.A. than New York. That simple. Met my wife here and started a life. I've lived in New York and adore it, and if we didn't have kids or if I was filthy rich then we'd be there.
—Xavier, actor, playwright, and screenwriter

I wanted to work as an actor in animation, so L.A. was the best market for that.
—Maya, actor and animation voice-over artist

I am based in L.A. instead of New York because at the time I moved, there was more work here. Now you have to be a dual citizen.

—Sammy, veteran actor and comedian

My wife won't move.

—Gavin, leading man and series regular on iconic TV show

The industry in New York is harder to crack—although I've learned that in L.A., landing a meeting just means they were scared not to meet with you—just in case you turned out to be "someone" down the road.

—Bethany, TV writer, show creator, and showrunner

I started out in New York, and bounced back and forth for years following the work. I think I eventually got used to the roomier spaces in L.A., and driving a car, and the weather. My hard New Yorker shell slipped off somewhere along the way.

—Jessica, TV and indie film producer

Having lived briefly in New York, I dislike the prospect of living in New York.

—Austin, playwright and comedy writer

You fly to L.A. You get in the pool. You get out, and you're fifty.

—Anonymous

If you want to be famous, I have nothing for you. But if you want to become a solid, grinding actor, then work on your craft as hard as you can; be diligent about classes.

—Carter, TV actor and series regular on a hugely popular show

4

IGNORANCE IS BLISS

———

Everybody Starts Somewhere

Not long ago, when I was teaching an audition workshop in New York, a young actor raised his hand and started asking questions about classes. I quickly discovered that he wasn't talking about (and had no real interest in) actual acting classes. His interest was exclusively focused on the audition workshops, now frequently being taught by casting directors and their associates, that focus exclusively on how to present yourself well in a professional audition situation. These classes have become hugely popular on both coasts because they place new actors directly in front of the very people who could potentially call them in for real paying work in the business. His questions basically came down to, "Why waste time and money taking old-fashioned acting classes when the instructor can't do anything to further my career?"

I told him what I tell everybody: audition workshops do provide a unique opportunity to be seen and hopefully get some practical advice from someone who watches a *lot* of auditions. I'm not opposed to them (in fact, I've taken a couple myself). My issue is that if you are not a strong actor, you will never be a strong auditioner. The young actor countered with a list of successful actors (no doubt culled from an exhaustive Google search) who had never taken acting class. They just "had it." They were "naturals," as he put it. A few minutes later, he got up to work. I take no pleasure in reporting that he did not "have it" nor was he "a natural." He was stiff as a poker and shouted his lines at the reader, with no clue what his character was actually struggling with at that moment in time. No casting director in their right mind would have called this young man in for an audition.

He radiated only one easily recognizable quality: impatience.

And he reminded me a little of myself.

By the time I had landed in New York, scored a place to live, found a job, and could stop to take a breath, almost seven months had passed. I was shocked when I realized how fast it had gone by. I needed to get going! After all, I had plans for myself. Very big plans. I needed to get an agent and maybe a manager (although I had no idea what a manager was at the time). I had Oscars, Emmys, and Tonys to win. There were red carpets to walk. Magazine covers to grace. And talk shows to appear on. I needed to get this party started.

And then it occurred to me that I had no idea how to do any of this. I'd come to New York because I sort of felt like I had "something," but I didn't know what it was. And whatever it was, it was highly undependable. Sometimes it was there, but sometimes it wasn't. And I was very scared by all the crazy stories I'd heard about megalomaniacal acting teachers in New York. Part of me didn't want to study acting for fear that it would screw up what I thought might be my natural genius.

Finally, I signed up for an inexpensive acting class held weekly in a small theatre in Greenwich Village. It was taught by a former actor who was now writing detective novels. He was a very nice guy who certainly had some experience, but his feedback tended to be kind of vague and anecdotal, and I soon got the feeling that teaching this class was probably just a way of keeping his rent paid while he wrote his books. During the time I was in his class, I did two scenes, and both times I had the same experience.

The format for the class gave you two cracks at your chosen scene. The first time you went up, you were on your own, and most of the students went down in flames. The instructor would then give you some guidance, and the following week you got another shot at the material. During my first attempt at any given scene, I always felt so nervous and unfocused that I could barely remember my lines. I was awful, and I knew it. After getting notes from the teacher, I'd then do a little half-assed rehearsing with my scene partner. These sessions usually consisted of very little actual work and mostly involved smoking a lot of cigarettes and complaining about our lives.

A week later, I'd be up in front of the class again. And that's when this weird thing would happen. As I climbed onto the stage, my whole body became filled with adrenaline. I'd feel hot and scared and like the top of my head was about to blow off. Then I'd look over at my scene partner, and it was as if I'd never seen her before. Suddenly, the scene would unexpectedly take on a life of its own. Lines were flying out of my mouth as freely as if they had wings. I felt like I was possessed. And then as quickly as it had begun, the scene was over, followed by an enthusiastic burst of applause from my classmates. In both instances, I was highly praised for having "discovered" the scene at the eleventh hour. On the one hand, I was grateful for the praise, since it made me feel that maybe I was a "natural." But on the other hand, I had no idea why or how I'd been able to cheat death again. Secretly, I felt like a total fraud.

There was an older actor in the class (meaning she was possibly thirty) who had an agent, went to real auditions, and frequently arrived late because she was always "coming from rehearsal." Just after leaving my final class, she confronted me on the sidewalk and gave me a cold, hard stare. She was a native New Yorker and had one of those accusatory gazes that make you feel like she'd caught you shoplifting or something.

"Are you for real?" she asked me.

"I'm sorry—what?"

"This whole 'country boy' shtick you do: Is it for real?"

"I'm sorry, I don't know what you're—"

"Do you know what you're doing or not?" she asked impatiently.

I sensed she was on the verge of possibly sharing something important with me, or maybe even offering me a leg up this mysterious ladder. I swallowed hard. "Uh, I don't know. Maybe . . ."

As my answer trailed off in a cloud of uncertainty, so did her interest. As she turned and walked away, she muttered, "Well, if you ever figure it out, you might have something."

My heart sank. Part of me wanted to yell after her, "Wait! I want to have 'something'! I want a rehearsal to go to. I want to return my agent's call. I want to walk on stage like I know what I'm doing!" But none of that came out of my mouth. My feet were glued to the sidewalk. I was a fake.

I was experiencing the beginning of everybody's true entrance into the life of being an artist. The moment when you realize that neither desire nor bravado will get you through the door. Only skill can do that.

Most people become attracted to acting, writing, or directing from sitting in the bleachers watching the major players do their thing. Our love for the craft comes from witnessing how these remarkable artists can move us, scare us, thrill us, or break our hearts. Even though we don't personally know these people, we experience strong feelings about them. They are the coolest human beings imaginable. Their art appears so seamless, organic, and perfect. The emotion they generate in us often marks the beginning of what will become, for many of us, a lifelong love affair with art and artists.

For those of you who truly believe this business is for you, the moment you realize you are *not yet ready* to join this club is the moment you truly start the initiation process.

The vast majority of actors, writers, and directors achieve their success by working their asses off. Yes, there are a select few who oddly buy one ticket and win the whole jackpot. No sooner do they set their suitcase down than an agent from CAA arrives at the bus station, contracts in hand. Personally, I tend to hate these people, but it's not really their fault that they are so irresistible. They just are. These instant success stories are, of course, legendary, and they are also extremely rare. Most people in show business have to "learn and earn" their way in. And that means staggering around in the dark for a while and squeezing through any door that will open even a crack.

This is a little hard to articulate, but everything you've seen that you loved—amazing performances, brilliant scripts, ingenious direction—was most likely first stumbled upon, then studied, then crafted, and then, in a moment of alchemy, magically "set free" to dazzle whoever was lucky enough to be in the audience. That freedom is the final result of a ton of work—usually *years* of work—that involves studying the emotional architecture of whatever art form you're currently obsessed with. It requires imagination. It requires tenacity. It requires a strong sense of truth. It requires skill—personal skill that is rooted in who you are as a human being. And skill is gained in only one way: through exploration and practice. Initially, failure will be your first and best teacher. Later, successes will start arriving, and they will have even more interesting lessons to teach you.

Long story short: The only way to find out who you are as an artist is to start finding out what you do—and how you do it. This is more fun than it sounds. But it involves being a willing, open-minded, courageous student of your craft. And you can start the process by learning from the best.

We live in an incredible time, when virtually everything is available online. Utilize this resource and start watching the artists you admire with new eyes. Don't watch them as a fan. Don't sit there intimidated and awed. Watch them as a student of whatever art they practice. There's method to their shimmering madness. In the end, each of us discovers and shapes our own individual formulas that allow us to access our unique talent (more on that later), but it begins by learning to see with new, discerning eyes.

But don't let watching others be your only education. You've got classes to take. *Acting* classes. You've got books to read. You've got some truly horrible art to create (while inching your way toward creating some excellent and interesting art). Most importantly, let those famous artists inspire you, fill you with wonder, and keep you going while you hunker down and start learning your craft—which is basically what I told that young man in my workshop.

By the way, I did not return to that acting class in the Village. I started asking around for recommendations for a new teacher, and soon a couple of names started coming up, over and over. Soon I found myself in a class with an instructor who demanded quite a lot more of me, and I had no choice but to run a little faster and jump a little higher just to keep up. It was scary, but it was also great. I slowly stopped being a clueless, erratic mess who didn't know who or what I was, and I started to become somebody.

There is freedom in admitting you know nothing. In that magic moment, you're released from cruel expectations and stupid comparisons. You're an empty, expectant, blank canvas on which (if you're genuinely talented) will soon appear a totally unique work of art.

Ready? Let's find you a teacher.

Seven true things for when you're just starting out:

1. We are all impatient. It's a fact. So learn to use your impatience constructively. Being impatient with the business's failure to recognize your brilliance is a waste of time. Instead, use that impatience to prioritize your work as an artist. Find out what you need to work on. Then work on it.

2. The beginning is a little confusing for everybody. So keep in mind that we all start somewhere. The best way to start is by learning how to listen. To yourself. And to the world around you. Listen carefully and often. Here's why:

3. It's *impossible* to be a good artist if you cannot truly listen and be affected and changed by what is coming at you. That takes practice. You must learn to listen *like an artist*. If you can't do that, you'll never *be* an artist.

4. Becoming a fan is also a terrific idea. Not just for young artists, but also for established artists looking to recharge their batteries. Becoming an avid observer of how great work is constructed is an excellent way to awaken or reawaken your awe of and love for the art form. Your idols can help you develop and define your identity as an artist and harness your talent.

5. You are entering a world where empires are built using just the imagination. It's an astoundingly powerful tool. Learn to engage yours daily. It's your raw material. It's the well from which everything will be drawn. Make sure it's deep and full. More on this later.

6. Humility is not the same thing as feeling inadequate. True humility is about honesty and a sincere willingness to find your specific place in this new world—a place that doesn't yet exist on any map. Only you can find it, because only you will recognize it.

7. You're now going to start figuring out what you want to know and who is teaching that particular thing. You are panning for gold. There will be a lot of dirt, but once it's washed away, you'll start to see something shiny and valuable.

My best teacher honored the mess in me and showed me how beautiful my flaws were. I learned courage and strength, physical power.

—Rachel, stage and TV actor

5

A CLASS ACT

———

Where to Study

I had been in New York for about a year when I first got wind of the legendary acting teacher William Esper. Bill was the heir apparent to the even more legendary Sanford Meisner, and getting into one of his classes was not easy. There was no audition process. Instead, you had to interview with him, and even getting the interview was tricky. Ambitious little bastard that I was, I started calling his studio and leaving numerous messages until finally a somewhat frosty assistant returned my call. Apparently, not just anybody got in to see this Esper guy. Only the "serious" need apply.

In those days I tended to meet attitude with even more attitude, so I made it plain that my intention was to schedule an interview with Mr. Bill Esper, not to be quizzed on my seriousness by some loser assistant. However, sensing I was about to be hung up on, I finally caved in and did a little song and dance about how dedicated I was to the craft of acting. Blah, blah, blah. Three days later I got a rather condescending voicemail from the assistant informing me that I'd been granted an audience the following Thursday and to be on time.

The real reason the assistant's attitude had bugged me so much was that I suspected there might well be some kind of barrier between me and this elite class of "serious" students, and I wanted desperately to crash through it. To my credit, I was a spunky kid, but my track record for actually finishing the things I started wasn't so great. The other problem was that I was working at a rather low-wage job and didn't even know how much the classes would cost. However, like Scarlett O'Hara, I decided I'd worry about that tomorrow. First things first.

When the day of my interview arrived, I wanted to make a solid impression, so I carefully dressed in the worst-looking T-shirt I owned, and jeans that had rips and paint stains on them. This was part of my newly minted young, I-don't-give-a-crap persona, and I felt sure it would make me look more "serious" in the eyes of Mr. Esper. I had also heard through the grapevine that he didn't take students under the age of twenty-three, so on the application they gave me to fill out, I lied about my date of birth, inching my age up to twenty-four (when I was in fact only twenty-one). In hindsight, I doubt anyone was fooled. At six feet tall I weighed, at the time, about 140 pounds and looked like I might be a junior in high school.

When my name was called, I was suddenly overcome with a case of jittery nerves. In those days, acting teachers in New York were almost required to have guru status, so I wasn't really sure what to expect. As it turned out, the mysterious Esper was a stocky, fiftyish man with glasses and a slight Cleveland accent. Seated behind his battered desk, he seemed more like a working-class regular Joe, a gentle soul who sort of reminded me of my father. I instantly relaxed when I discovered that the interview had nothing to do with the lofty art of acting. Instead, it merely consisted of a series of easy-to-answer questions, like, Where was I from? How long had I lived in New York? How did I like the city? In fact, it all seemed too easy. I began to get suspicious.

Feeling I needed to make a stronger impression, I started steering the conversation toward my lofty goals as an artist, and how much I admired the work of Chekhov and Strindberg (two playwrights I had never actually read) and how badly I wanted to get into this class. Bill smiled patiently, and instead of addressing any of my remarks, got down to brass tacks. The class met twice a week. I would be expected to put in rehearsal time with my scene partner, and the class would cost $160 a month. Would I be able to afford that? A small knot formed in my stomach as I remembered that I barely had the subway fare to get home from this interview.

I smiled weakly. "Yes, sure," I lied. "No problem."

Then my potential new instructor shifted his weight back into his chair and looked directly into my eyes. It was the first time I experienced the legendary "Esper stare." Hard to describe; I can only say that Bill could, without uttering a single word, clearly convey the message *Let's cut the bullshit here.*

"Why do you want to be an actor?" he asked.

Out of all the questions he could have asked me, this was the one I was least pre-pared to answer. Terror swept over me. A lump formed in my throat. I was getting my first taste of why Bill was such a tremendous teacher. It wasn't so much *what* he had asked me, but *how* he had said it. Suddenly, the question had enormous weight. Here I was, asking for admission into the world of being a "serious art-ist," and I'd never been serious about anything in my life. Now I was being asked the big question, the one that would determine everything. I felt like I was on an elevator that was rapidly plummeting to the bottom of my twenty-one-year-old soul—a place, I would later learn, where all truth is stored. Realizing I could stall no longer, I cleared my throat. My voice cracked as a completely unexpected answer came out of my mouth: "Because I don't like being myself."

A small, almost imperceptible smile curled up the corners of Bill's mouth. I couldn't tell if he was pleased or bemused by my answer. Turning his eyes back to my application, he scribbled a note in the margin and mumbled something about how his assistant would be contacting all the applicants later in the week about who would be admitted into the class.

Clearly, my interview was over, but I couldn't move. For the first time in my young life, I'd genuinely revealed myself, but I had no idea whether it had helped or hurt my cause. Unable to take the suspense, I asked, "Did I get in?"

Bill gave me a fatherly, noncommittal smile and extended his hand. "We'll see."

The walk from his desk to the office door seemed like an eternity. I had never felt so relieved to hear a door click shut behind me.

Two days later, I received a call from the now less-haughty assistant. I had been accepted into Bill's class and would start my training as a professional actor the following week. I felt like I had won the lottery! That is, until the assistant reminded me that in this particular sweepstakes, I would be the one paying them. A check for $160 would be due on the first day of class. Within the hour, I had booked an extra shift at work and was soon calling everyone I knew to brag about my victory. That night I celebrated with Top Ramen and a beer. I had separated myself from the pack. I was *serious* now.

The two years I spent attending classes in Bill's studio (located three floors above a strip joint on 7th Avenue) shaped everything I know about acting and, later in my career, writing and directing. The training consisted of defining a series of skill sets that gradually built on each other until they finally (if you were smart and had talent) led you to a fully realized performance.

There were times when I was terrified of failing, but I always opted to trust Bill completely. I can remember having to do an exercise using an object, and my task was to create a set of circumstances that made the object very valuable to me. I happened to have in my possession a pair of old wire-rimmed eyeglasses that had once belonged to my grandfather, a man who'd died before I was born, but someone I'd often wondered about. The circumstance I created was that my father had lent them to me for an audition and I had accidentally damaged them. During the exercise, I had to speak and interact with another actor while trying to repair the damaged spectacles. Something about the fragility of the glasses and the fear of my father's disappointment triggered something utterly unexpected, and I became flooded with emotion. Tears began to slowly roll down my face, falling onto my hands and onto the spectacles. I continued talking, continued trying to deal with the onslaught coming from the other actor, until Bill eventually stopped the exercise. His initial words were for the other actor—and they were a bit blunt. Then he spoke to me, and in a gentler tone simply said: "You're a good student. That was okay."

If I had been handed an Academy Award at that moment, I could not have felt prouder. What had just happened in that classroom did not feel to me like "acting." It had been a human experience that had been crafted. Using everything I'd been taught up to that time, I had managed to open the door between the real world and an imaginary one, and for a few precious minutes I had slipped through to the other side. It was exhilarating, and now, more than anything, I wanted to know more.

My time in Bill Esper's studio taught me the best lesson any class can offer: how to teach myself. He carefully, methodically walked me and my classmates through the process by which we could train our imaginations to serve us. He instilled confidence that our talent, if accessed truthfully, could set us free under any circumstance we might find ourselves in. He instilled in us that this choice to work within imaginary circumstances would lead to greater freedom and that our understanding would only deepen with time and practice. In short, if we served the truth, we would only become better.

Choosing which acting school to attend means figuring out what sort of program interests you and will meet your needs. Are you looking to be a full-time student working toward a degree? Do you want to be in a conservatory program that will give you training not just in acting but also movement, voice, and the classics?

Are you the sort of individual who thrives in a structured environment? Or do you feel drawn toward studying in a smaller studio, or with a particular teacher who uses a specific methodology? There are no right or wrong answers. You need to consider what is the best fit for you, your goals, your location, and your bank account. There are many wonderful places (and ways) to learn your craft. (For me, the more structured world of a university program did not work well for a number of reasons: some personal, some artistic, and some financial.) And keep in mind that attending a school with famous alumni is no guarantee of anything.

Wherever you study, you should focus on creating a solid base that readies you for the day you will leave the safety of the nest and fly with your own wings. Acting, writing, and directing are all unique art forms, but each contains a secret code, an invisible structure—a treasure map, if you will—that a wonderful teacher can help you discover. Make sure you don't leave after the first discovery. More discoveries will follow. Hang in there until you are bursting with ideas of your own.

Be wary of classrooms where the emphasis seems to be on the glories of the past. Any good class is about today and what might happen tomorrow. If your teacher is not installing skills into you, offering you keys that unlock doors, and ultimately readying you for your day of departure, then you're with the wrong teacher.

If you flip to the Resources section in the back of this book, you'll find a handy list of established schools and teachers based in New York and L.A. They all cost money. There are many, many more options beyond the ones listed. Keep looking until you find a school, studio, or teacher you're truly excited about. Be aware that if a school (particularly a conservatory) describes their program as "rigorous," they're not kidding. Choose wisely!

Eight ways to know whether you're in the right school or class:

1. Do you feel at home in the classroom? It's tough to learn anything in a class where you feel intimidated or out of place. The atmosphere of any class is largely dictated by the instructor. Does the instructor create an atmosphere that instills trust and courage among the students?

2. What is being taught in the class? If you were asked to, could you articulate what you are learning? In theory, you should be gaining skills that will work for you outside the classroom. What techniques will you be taking with you? If you can't clearly identify what is being taught, this might not be a good class for you.

3. Good schools tend to attract good students. Do your fellow students appear to be talented, curious individuals who are committed to growing and sharpening their skills?

4. I've heard some horror stories from students who spent precious time and money in a class that seemed to be more about the teacher than about the students. Be wary of classes that appear to be cultish or designed to flatter the ego of the instructor. Also look out for frequent and lengthy anecdotes about famous people. The focus of any class should always be on the work of the artists who are present, not on the work of icons who are not.

5. A good class should make you feel differently about your work. When artists are learning and improving, the way in which they *experience* their art becomes more interesting and fun. Is that happening? If not, perhaps you need a different class.

6. Finding an instructor or school that fits you is a little like dating, so shop around before you commit. Talk to others. Do some research. Try to audit classes before signing up. If you have a bad feeling about joining a class, pay attention to that instinct.

7. Instructors have different methods, but the bottom line should always be that the person is as passionate and committed to the craft as you are!

8. Praise is nice, but a good teacher should always be pushing you to do better. That's their job.

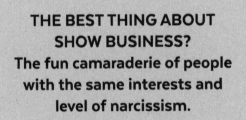

**THE BEST THING ABOUT
SHOW BUSINESS?
The fun camaraderie of people
with the same interests and
level of narcissism.**

—Laurence, iconic theatre performer and playwright

6

PICTURE THIS

———

Capturing the Perfect Headshot

About once a year, I go through the pile of business cards that have wound up in the top drawer of my desk. I routinely toss most of them into the recycling bin because I no longer have any idea who these people are or where I met them. The 10 percent I do hang onto have one thing in common: they all include a photograph of the person's face. As soon as I see the face, I remember the person and the conversation. A photo is a tiny but potent representation of the human being associated with it.

In the olden times, only actors had to worry about having a headshot. Directors, writers, designers, producers, and the remaining army of professionals that make up show business didn't have to worry about having a photo of themselves to catch the attention of the job-givers. You lived or died on the strength of your resume. Well, times have changed. We all now live in an ultrafast, online, visually oriented world where the competition for employment has never been more fierce.

My serious advice is to have at least one terrific photo that represents you, and it needs to be on anything that's promoting your name and credentials: your resume, your website, your business cards, your email signature. In essence, your image—accompanied by your job title and other pertinent information—needs to be in the widest circulation possible.

Although I know it's a part of my job, I hate having my picture taken. I'm not particularly photogenic. I'm not fishing for compliments here. I don't think I'm a hideous toad or anything, but for some reason the camera and I rarely seem to get along.

For starters, I have a somewhat asymmetrical face, which I don't really mind in life, but it always looks sort of weird to me when frozen on film. When I'm forced to look at multiple shots of myself, suddenly nothing is to my liking. My features are either too big or too small, too high or too low, too close together or too far apart. Photographs also rob me of my most treasured illusion: that I'm still a young, up-and-coming person in show business; that I'm just a kid with my whole life ahead of me. These days, there's a somewhat more mature set of eyes gazing back at me from the JPEGs.

In the early days of my career, I always ordered far too many copies of my head-shots. It wasn't so much a case of narcissism as it was a desperate attempt to define myself in some way. Being young, I didn't really know who I was or what kind of actor I wanted to be. While one shot seemed to reveal my funny, lovable side, another made me look sort of intense and angry, and yet another suggested I could do sad, waifish characters. Since I naturally wanted to play *all* of those roles someday, I assumed that the best plan was to order fifty copies of each look. Of course, no agent I ever worked with really wanted more than two or three shots.

In those days, I was also obsessed with finding the "right" photographer. If I could somehow make a perfect artist-to-artist connection, then that person's camera would at long last reveal my as-yet-untapped brilliance! This led to a couple of expensive disasters along the way. Once I showed up (with my eight changes of clothing) and was met at the door by a loopy photographer who instantly pro-claimed that I looked "waaay too tense." Looking back, I should have been a little suspicious, since she was drinking a glass of wine at eleven o'clock in the morning, but I was a little green back then. Somehow, I let her talk me into getting stoned before the session. It would "loosen me up," she promised. She was in posses-sion of some killer weed, and all I remember is laughing my ass off for the next two hours and thinking how these pictures were going to be totally awesome! However, when I got the prints, my eyes were half-closed and I looked utterly and completely baked. When I showed them to my agent, he remarked, "Well, these will be great if Cheech and Chong ever do another movie."

Having sat in the director's chair a couple of times in my life, I can tell you that when it comes to headshots, simple accuracy is helpful. One common mistake actors make is choosing a hugely flattering shot. That's all fine and good if you happen to be drop-dead gorgeous. But if you're a regular "nice-looking" person, you need to be prepared for some sighs of disappointment when you walk in the door. This is show business. If they are looking for serious eye candy, believe you me, they can find it.

The second most common mistake is even deadlier. When you hand a potential employer your headshot, the last thing you want them to be thinking is, *When exactly was this taken?* Show business is pretty much obsessed with youth and, like it or not, almost everyone in the business has a pretty keen eye. If you submit a photo that looks like it was taken ten years ago, the first question uttered after you leave the room will be, "How old do you think he/she is?"

When I teach young actors, I try to stress that they develop a strong personal sense of truth. And truth is definitely something you want to have in play when deciding how to represent yourself. All any of us needs is two or three appealing photographs that actually look like us. In a perfect world, those pictures also convey the only things of value any of us have to offer the artistic process: our personality, our humor, our beauty, and our flaws. In short, our actual honest-to-God selves.

Many of my students ask me to look at their photos. The task of picking the "right ones" is very confusing. Will this one work for this medium? Will that one work for another? If they have an agent, I try to defer these questions to the person who will actually be submitting the actor for work.

If they are not being represented, I look for a photo that contains either mystery or appeal. What do I mean by that? Here's what:

Consider Leonardo da Vinci's masterwork, the *Mona Lisa*. For centuries, people have been trying to decipher the meaning or message being delivered by her enigmatic smile and the expression in her eyes. She has remained steadfastly mysterious yet intriguing. Her image generates a feeling when gazed at. You are curious about this woman. You would like to know more. That is the quality that your photo should convey. Simply put, it should capture a moment when something is going on in your face, your eyes, your mind, your heart, that makes the onlooker interested in meeting this person. It makes them think, *I'd like to know more.*

Renowned photographer Annie Leibovitz once said, "When I photograph someone, what it really means is that I want to get to know them." That's a lovely sentiment, and one that I suspect is true for many photographers. So the next time somebody points a camera at you, don't flinch. Open your whole self up and let them in. Give 'em the whole picture.

Nine things to keep in mind about your headshots:

1. The price of a photo session can vary widely, from a couple hundred to a couple thousand. If you know someone is a good amateur photographer, you may not need to pay big bucks for headshots. But make sure you sit down together and look at professional actor headshots online, so you both truly understand what you need. There are a lot of photographers out there, so if you can afford a professional, shop around. If you need a little help with this decision, ask a fellow actor (preferably someone who's got a little more experience than you). If your budget is tight, don't make an expensive mistake.

2. Get a full night's sleep prior to the session. Never show up hung over or exhausted.

3. Don't wear clothing with crazy patterns or stripes. No logos. Keep the clothing as neutral as possible. You want them looking at *you*. Not the clothes.

4. You don't need to print a zillion different "looks." For most actors, a "dramatic" (nonsmiling shot) and a "comedic" (smiling) shot will do it. Since you're trying to establish your identity with the show business community, don't flood the market with a truckload of different-looking photos of yourself. If there's a particular kind of role that you're going after, you might have another shot, like a "business exec" picture (in different clothing), or if you're sexy, you might want a "hot" shot that subtly but clearly conveys that quality. If you are repped, speak with your agent and ask them what they need, and ask their opinion before you print anything. Don't make them look at two hundred options. Pick the finalists, and then invite them into the final selection process.

5. Many casting directors will be looking at your photo online—that usually means they'll be seeing a very small thumbnail version of it. Make sure your photo still pops in that format. Discuss colors and clothing choices with your photographer so you wind up with an image that's effective and eye-catching at any size.

6. Even though most submissions are handled digitally these days, you'll still need hard copies of your headshot, especially at the beginning of your career. These are for mailings to agents and casting directors, and auditions for showcases (aka nonpaying shows that give you a chance to hone your performing skills and maybe get seen by an agent or casting director).

7. Make sure these photos are also part of your social media presence. But don't overdo it. They represent your brand (aka your professional identity), but not your whole life. Social media should give a picture of you as a well-rounded, living, breathing person.

8. Everybody under the age of thirty always laughs at me when I pull out a business card with my face and info on it. Let 'em laugh. The cards work. Yes, I can easily type my name and number into somebody's cell, but when I do that, I pretty much instantly disappear into their massive list of contacts. A card requires the person to actually look at it the next day and remember our conversation.

9. If you're going to pursue modeling, print work, or commercials (which a lot of actors do), those areas require somewhat more specific photos. Ask your agent what you need and make sure you provide it.

**To succeed in show business, you
need determination, persistence,
talent, a network . . . and *rage*.**

—Jeremiah, leading man, musician, and
series regular on iconic TV series

7

THE FRIEND ZONE

———

Starting Your Network

One day early in my career, I picked up a message informing me that one of the zillion resumes I'd mailed out had actually been looked at, and now a small Equity theatre company wanted to see me for a show they were producing. I was to come in and read for a role in a revival of a play called *Hard to Be a Jew* by Sholem Aleichem (whose stories about Tevye the dairyman were the basis for a little musical called *Fiddler on the Roof*). The role I was auditioning for was a young man who, although Jewish, could pass for a gentile.

In case I didn't mention this earlier, I am from rural Eastern Kentucky, where (when I was growing up) there were maybe five black people and, to my knowledge, no Jews. In fact, I had not known there were any Jewish people in America until I was about nineteen years old. I had made Jewish friends while in Texas, and many more since moving to New York. In fact, my new best buddy from acting class was a very talented guy about my age (also named David) who happened to be Jewish. I quickly read the play and understood none of it. Well, that's not true. I understood the plot, but I didn't understand any of the jokes or the relationships or the historical context of a single event in the script.

Nonetheless, I marched down to the theatre the following day to audition for *Hard to Be a Jew*. As I sat in the waiting room, which was filled with actors much more appropriate for this play than I was, I felt like the world's biggest goy. Finally,

I read, and everyone present politely thanked me for coming in. As I walked out of the theatre, I wasn't mad or disappointed. All I wanted was to find the nearest pay phone. Using one of the precious quarters I was saving to do my laundry, I dialed my friend David.

"Get your butt down here!" I told him.

"I can't!" he replied miserably. "I don't have an appointment. It would be too weird."

"Don't be an idiot!" I yelled at him. "You gotta come *now*! Grab your resume and get down here. They are looking for *you*!"

He did. As I predicted, they granted him an audition. And because David was (and still is) an awesome actor, he booked a role in *Hard to Be a Jew*, which was his first professional gig in New York.

I'm telling you this story not to prove what a nice guy I am or how talented my friend is, but to demonstrate the importance of having a network.

Probably the biggest misconception about working in entertainment is that it's some kind of solitary pursuit. Let me tell you, it's anything but. It takes a village. If you want to get anywhere, you will need a network. And in order to assemble your network, you will need to do some networking. But who or what makes up a network? And where do you find these people?

If you are in the beginning of your career, then you are at the beginning of your network. That means it will be made up of the people you know from college, your acting class, and your gym, or just friends you will make on the usual social circuit of young artists. At this stage of your life you are unlikely to run into a big producer or agent at that BYOB party in Eagle Rock or Bed-Sty. However, be aware that even in these early days you could wind up sitting next to someone who, ten years hence, may wield power in the business, so it pays to say hello and be friendly at every opportunity.

Your network should always be an ever-evolving group of people with whom you have some kind of relationship—which means they would recognize your name if they heard it. If this individual couldn't pick you out of a lineup, they are not yet in your network. And in theory, you and the people in your network will share information and help each other out in the same way mentioned in my *Hard to Be a Jew* story. Maintaining a productive network also means you must continually be adding talented, active, ambitious, and (of course) successful people to your address book at every opportunity.

For years, I was mortified by the idea of doing this. It always conjured up an image of me marching up to someone and launching into some hideously embarrassing brown-nosing session. But throughout my career I've known people who are phenomenal at networking. I have a good friend who, even when we were youngsters, could work a room like she'd just won two Tonys and an Oscar. Virtually every conversation ended with her saying, "We should get together and talk about that." And because she is gorgeous and smart as a whip, largely people were (and continue to be) willing to do exactly that. As a result, she is rarely out of work.

Another character actor friend of mine never leaves a job without collecting contact info from every potential job-giver. Then, when he discovers that that individual is working again, he's immediately in touch and very direct about his desire for a job. When I asked him where he got his courage to do things like that, he replied, "I have kids. This has to work out."

For a moment I considered running out and adopting some kids, but then I thought better of it. However, his phrase "This has to work out" stuck with me. He was right. Since this is, after all, my chosen profession, I couldn't just sit on my butt and pretend that this aspect of it wasn't important.

So, since I'm not gorgeous or ballsy, I began to consider the most authentic way I could approach networking. I do like going to events. I like meeting new people, and unless they are hugely standoffish, I like asking them about themselves and their work. I've always been interested in what others are doing. And if it's an artist who does work I admire, I have no problem telling them so. If someone I think is truly talented is doing something (a live show, a screening of their short movie, a reading of their script), I usually try to show up and support them.

So I decided that instead of trying to be a networker, I'd become a supporter. And if I was going to approach somebody, I wasn't going to ask; I was going to offer.

Translation: If the opportunity arose to speak to somebody with some talent or some clout, I was going to open with a truthful, sincere compliment or observation about them, their work, or something else that I knew was meaningful to them. And I'm happy to report that this policy has worked out really well for me. A little sincerity might (or might not) open up an opportunity to have a fun, genuine conversation. If it doesn't, I can walk away with my head held high, since nothing embarrassing happened.

I'll add some other tips at the end of this chapter, but here's the big point:

Every actor, writer, director, producer, casting person, agent, or manager you talk to is also a human being. Depending on the circumstances in which you encounter them, they might be receptive to a little chat, but probably not a thinly disguised pitch or vague request for help. They probably already have a nightstand piled with scripts and an inbox jammed with requests from people they already know. As soon as they see where this is going, you'll probably get a glassy-eyed stare as they start looking for the nearest exit.

If your remark is sincere and well-observed, it will contain references or adjectives that will connect the person to what they love about their work (to which they've given a healthy portion of their life). And the love of work might be the only thing the two of you have in common.

Think about it.

It can make a difference. Not always, but sometimes it truly works—if you are sincere. There are also a few ways of framing that remark that can leave the door open for the potential job-giver to say, "Thanks for the kind words. And what are you doing?"

Just keep in mind that in order to effectively network, you have to find a way to make it a fun experience for yourself. Whatever system you're going to use, make sure it fits your personality. If you are the world's greatest schmoozer, love hustling up party invitations, and can really work the room, then go for it! If you are a somewhat more reserved personality, then figure out how to volunteer your services in such a way that you'll be forced to talk with other people in the industry. A friend of mine started working the check-in table at industry events and met a ton of people that way. Other friends have volunteered their services to union committees or charities associated with the industry. And don't forget the fun stuff. Play on an industry-based softball team or start a poker game with your most talented friends. You can come up with something.

Four final thoughts about networking:

1. The goal of networking is to (a) meet new people in your industry, (b) get reacquainted with people you already know, and (c) find out about projects and opportunities firsthand—ideally from the people who are creating them.

2. Networking is personal contact. Face to face. Or at least a phone conversation. If a potential job-giver "likes" your Instagram post, that's a good start, but I wouldn't necessarily say they are a part of your network just yet. Your goal should always be human contact. Electronic messages are not without value, but they are very easily forgotten. Face-to-face interaction means you are on the person's radar. Always shoot for that.

3. If you are still resistant to the idea of networking, reframe your thinking. For me, it helps to remember that when I attend an event I am there to support those I admire, love, or have history with, as much as I am there to meet new people and see what's going on in my industry. I'm not there asking for a favor, a loan, or a handout. I'm there because I'm also an active member of this ever-churning, ever-surprising, very fun community. That's it. If I'm not insincere, then nobody will accuse me of that crime. So go start making friends. And offer them what you've got.

4. Networking, at its core, means being out among the living. You don't have to do it obsessively or insincerely, but you need to do it. We all do.

Be tough and stay committed to your dreams. And treat it as a business.

—Richard, veteran Hollywood talent agent

8

PERFECT STRANGERS

————

What Is an Agent?

My first agents were Marla and Diane, two lovely middle-aged ladies who commuted in from the suburbs each day on a mission to get their clients work in the glamorous world of New York theatre. They had a modest little office on the corner of West 57th Street and 8th Avenue and tended to represent a lot of young hopefuls like me on a freelance basis (so it was a loose arrangement at best). Once in a while, I would swing by unannounced with a box of Fanny Farmer chocolates from the pharmacy downstairs, and they would act like I'd brought them diamonds from Tiffany's. I'm not sure how effective they were as agents, but they loved their clients with a passion. Anytime I needed an ego boost, all I had to do was stick my head in the door. According to Marla and Diane, I was the cutest, most talented, funniest, most charming young man in all of New York. How did I stay so skinny? And look at that smile! And my hair! Did I know how many women would kill to have hair that particular shade of blond? I never got much work from Marla and Diane, but I always left their office feeling like a million bucks. When they finally closed their doors, I moved to another joint staffed by younger agents who appeared to have a lot of energy, some of which seemed to be chemically engineered (it was the '80s).

Eventually, one of the energetic agents migrated to L.A. When I called to congratulate him on the move, he enthusiastically offered to represent me if I wanted to come out for pilot season (a brief period from January to March when all the new TV series are cast). Unfortunately, by the time I arrived, he'd sobered up and had no memory whatsoever of that conversation. I was screwed. I'd already sublet my apartment in New York and now found myself standing on Mars with no escape pod. Frantically, I sent out photos to a long list of L.A. agents that I knew nothing about. Finally, I got a call from a nice-sounding lady who asked me to stop by the following day. When I arrived, I discovered that she worked out of her home—her living room, to be precise. "Ginny" met me at the front door, wearing a bright red track suit. She invited me into her extremely messy living room and told me to have a seat. I moved a stack of 8 by 10s off the nearest chair and sat down. During our chat, Ginny (who was about sixty and a chain-smoker) told me that she'd recently gotten four of her clients jobs as "crew members" in a submarine movie that was currently shooting. In time, her husband, "Jimmy" (also dressed in a track suit), wandered in from the kitchen carrying a glass of tomato juice. Tossing a stack of manila envelopes out of the recliner, Jimmy sat down and joined the conversation. According to Jimmy, business had been "shit" last year, but things were definitely looking up. After about a half hour, I made up a lie about having another appointment and ducked out. I stayed in L.A. for three more months (agentless) until I finally gave up and retreated to New York.

Two years later, I was back. A play I'd cowritten was being done in Hollywood, and I was quickly discovering that producing theatre on the West Coast was a very different beast. Despite the fact that this was only a ninety-nine-seat, showcase production, the producers were obsessed with getting a "name" female actor for one of the plum character roles. Since there was no money involved, all we had to offer was a solid, funny part that the actor could use to attract a little industry attention. In other words, we had to find a slightly famous older woman who hadn't worked in a while. Even then, it was hard to get past the candidates' agents. Finally, I was dispatched by the producers to hand-deliver a copy of the script to an agent who was known for representing stars from yesteryear. She too worked out of her house, but hers was in the Hollywood Hills. I arrived and rang the bell but got no response. After a moment, I rang again.

"Hello?" a frail voice answered.

I was instantly alarmed. The voice (vaguely female) sounded like the speaker was 150 years old. I identified myself as the playwright who was dropping off a script for her client. I waited.

"Hello," the little voice croaked again. Not only was this woman 150, she was clearly deaf.

I started over, now yelling my whole explanation through the door, careful to slowly enunciate each word. Again, no response. Impatiently, I rang the bell again. Suddenly, I heard a scary sound. It was like a moan, or the kind of exhalation you make when experiencing a sharp pain. Panic swept over me as I pictured this poor elderly agent lying semiconscious in the hallway with a broken hip.

I knocked urgently on her door. "Excuse me!" I called. "Are you all right?"

Then I heard a distinct, unmistakable squawk. The agent was not home. I was talking to her parrot.

Trust me when I tell you there is a deep level of irony in this story that you will understand only after you've been in the business for a few years. Suffice to say, there will be times when you will think you are talking to someone in authority when in fact you are talking to a parrot.

Eventually, I settled into L.A. and began to find my way as a writer. Over time, I've had the good fortune to be represented by some very large and powerful agencies. This chapter of my life started when a script I'd written (and was shoving into the hands of any human being willing to read it) eventually landed on the desk of an executive at a major studio, who fortunately really loved it. When he discovered I didn't have an agent, he picked up the phone, and a week later I was signed to an agency that didn't just have an office. They had a building. A rather big building (more on that later). I wish I could say something wise and pithy about my experience playing with the big boys, but truthfully, other than the money and celebrities involved, my job (sitting at my desk, writing scripts) remained exactly the same as it was working with mid-level agencies, and my day-to-day experience wasn't that much different.

In reality, agents are not our fairy godparents—although there are times when I think they would truly like to be. Agents are not Santa or the tooth fairy either. They are salespeople trying to sell a mysterious commodity called talent. And talent is a living, breathing, ever-changing, sometimes crazy-making thing. The industry expects agents, as salespeople, to be in touch with the latest trends (even the tacky stupid ones) and not to waste anybody's time trying to move merchandise that's not currently in style. And agents need product that (even if it's not new) at least looks new. The greatest quality an agent can possess is tenacity.

One of my problems early on was that I failed to understand that an agent is not an accessory. They are real people with real lives, who (like their clients) are also obsessed with show business. They love TV, movies, and theatre. And they love artists, although I'm sure there are days when they also want to strangle them.

If you think being an artist is tough, imagine the pressure (both financial and emotional) that agents can find themselves under. Agents spend almost their entire day on the phone, trying to get appointments for their clients and (on good days) negotiating the best deals they can get for the clients that have booked work. The best agents work incredibly hard and are deeply frustrated when they're unable to move their clients' careers forward. They are also in business, and if they cannot move the merchandise (no matter how much they love it) they may need to end their relationship with that client. Agents often move mountains to build a performer's career, and then, when that performer scores a major career-changing job, the actor often leaves for a bigger, more prestigious office with a more star-studded list.

I've always done my best to stick by any agent who chose to rep me. In some cases, I had to move on because the office was unable to generate appointments. Who knows? In some cases I might have left too soon. In other cases I should have left six months before I did.

After the parrot episode, I called the elderly agent who had not been home to check on her client's availability. Unfortunately, the woman we were interested in had just been offered a dinner theatre show in Florida, but the agent had a couple of other clients she could suggest. Quickly, she began to rip through her list of older ladies—several of whom I was surprised to hear were still alive. None of them sounded quite right, so I politely declined. Then, as if she was playing her trump card, the agent triumphantly announced, "I can get you Rhonda Fleming." I had only a vague memory of Rhonda Fleming as a glamorous, red-haired bombshell from the early 1950s. Not exactly the gal to play a repressed, bible-thumping, Southern battle-ax. But I couldn't help but admire her agent's chutzpah. It made me hope that someday (even if it's a hundred-to-one shot), some intrepid rep will be willing to say, "I can get you David Dean Bottrell." Pause. "Yes, he's still alive."

Eleven facts about agents:

1. Their goal is to solicit work for their clients and to negotiate contracts for them.

2. Agents will submit your photo and resume to casting directors (professionals hired by the producers of a stage play, TV show, or film to assemble the best group of actors possible for the project). Please note: Casting directors decide only who will get an audition. They do not decide who is cast. Although they frequently campaign heavily for actors they believe in, the final decision on who gets the job rests with the director (who will

be working with the actors) and the producer(s) (who will be paying the actors).

3. Currently, agents charge a 10-percent commission on any job you book through them. Read your contract before signing it, because some offices now request a commission on any or all earnings (whether they were involved or not).

4. Every agent has their own style. How they run their day-to-day operations is their business, not yours. This is important because . . .

5. Results are the only thing you want from your agent.

6. Agencies come in all sizes. Bigger is not necessarily better. You may change agents during your career. You may not. It is ultimately your decision.

7. Some artists have very cordial relationships with agents. Others rarely speak with them—especially now that email has become the preferred method of communication. I suggest you foster the best, most communicative relationship you can create with your rep.

8. Your agent can only represent what you are giving them to represent. Make sure your product is terrific and up-to-date. Agents need talent that will always be dependable, flexible, and highly professional.

9. Agents have bills to pay. The clients that make more money are going to receive a bit more of the agents' attention. That doesn't mean they love their other clients any less.

10. If you don't make the agent money, they might drop you. If they do, don't use that as an excuse to beat yourself up. Just move on. If you are talented, skilled, and proactive, you'll eventually land somewhere else.

11. In the end, show business is just that—a business.

Stay authentic. Embrace your individuality. Embrace who you are.

—Marilyn, veteran talent manager

9

THE DATING GAME

How to Find an Agent

When I was a young actor in New York, I was painfully obsessed with the goal of signing an actual contract with an agent. To me it was the ultimate endorsement that clearly labeled me as a *professional*! Ironically, I worked for the first three years of my career without an agent, through the kindness of a couple of casting directors. In general, casting directors in New York tend to go to the theatre with some regularity, and in those days if they saw you in a play and liked your work, they'd call you in for an interview. These meetings didn't happen often for me, but when they did, it could sometimes wind up with my getting my name on their call list, which meant when a role came up that I was right for they would simply contact me directly—as opposed to going through an agent. Although I was able to get a few agents (like Marla and Diane) to "freelance" me through this period of my career, I didn't sign an actual contract with an agent until five years after I first landed in New York.

There are usually three ways that an agent will become interested in representing you.

1. They just fall in love with you. They have a feeling or an instinct that you have a healthy career ahead of you, and they want to lay claim to bragging rights that they were the first rep in town to spot that potential and the first to fight hard to get you on the map.

2. You have already started to book work on your own. You have at least a decent leg up in the industry, and there are already some casting offices that know you and your work. In this scenario, the agent is not utterly starting from scratch.

3. You are an established, well-known professional with a solid reputation who is leaving another agency in search of new representation. Usually, that means that you feel it's time to upgrade your reps based on how your career is going, or you feel that the current agency is simply not being well run.

People (both frustrated established players and newbies) often ask me if I can introduce them to my agency. I've tried that, but so far it has never worked. It's a lot like trying to fix two people up on a blind date. The chances are about a billion to one. I know this sounds bizarre, but when it comes to representation, it has to be love.

And believe me, you want it to be love. That love will cause your rep to push harder and plead more passionately to get you an appointment with a producer or casting director. It will also embolden your rep to fight harder for better money or billing for you when you hit the employment jackpot. That love is important and should not be taken for granted. If they don't feel that kind of enthusiasm for you and your talent, you don't want them to represent you.

And how do you find these people? Send them your picture and resume, accompanied by a very brief note. They might like your resume, but usually something about your gorgeous face, quirky smile, or brooding eyes must intrigue the rep enough that they will want to bring you in for an interview. However, the best way to enter an agent's office is through a recommendation from a casting director or a manager.

This seems like an opportune moment to talk about managers. While agents are primarily salespeople, managers tend to work with talent in a different way. Their job is to develop your career. They often sign talent early on and help with all the mechanics of launching and establishing your brand in the industry (this includes finding you an agent). That is important, because managers are not legally allowed to solicit work or negotiate contracts (although many are involved in both). In short, their job is to help you figure out a game plan and assist you in implementing it.

Management is hard to define because managers all do their jobs very differently. Some are deeply involved in their clients' lives. Some are more gatekeepers, guardians, and counselors. Managers tend to have fewer clients than agents and tend to do more hand-holding than agents can. Managers' commissions usually range between 10 percent and 15 percent of their clients' earnings. Make sure you read, understand, and agree with all terms before you sign a contract with a manager.

More and more, young actors can also gain access to agents through casting workshops—for a price. These workshops allow actors to audition for casting directors and agents, who then give them feedback on their work. Although for legal reasons these programs must be kept strictly educational, once you have met someone who feels like a good fit, you can reach out afterward to see if they have any interest in representing you. Casting workshops can easily be found online; they vary widely in format, reputation, and price, so shop around.

If you score an interview with an agent (or a manager), use that time to show them who you are—as a human being. If you are funny, show them that. If you are smart and observant, show them that. If you are curious about the world, show them that. If you a mess, show them that, but make sure it's an entertaining mess, not a scary mess. Just tell them the truth.

If they are interested, they will want to see more of your work, so be prepared. If you're an actor, can you do a monologue on demand? Do you have a reel posted online with video clips of your work? Are you singing at a local club? Are you doing stand-up or sketch somewhere? Are you appearing in a play somewhere soon? Reps tend to be busy people, so don't get your hopes up, but if they show up to see you, it's a pretty safe bet that they are seriously interested in working with you.

In some cases, the agent may have seen your work in advance and already know they want to rep you. In other cases, they will know instantly that they do not want to rep you and will politely wrap up the meeting.

If you begin a relationship with an agent, remember that this person is not a magician. They don't just tap you with their wand and you're immediately part of the club. Having a rep is a very good start, but it's just a start. They will now start trying to score appointments for you with potential employers. This can take time, so be patient.

Be aware that this is not the time to sit on your hands waiting for a call. This is a time to double down on whatever got you the attention of this person to begin with. Grab every opportunity to do your thing, and keep your agent apprised of whatever is happening. Show business is one of the few businesses on the planet where talk is not cheap. Your agent is now in a major battle to grab the attention of some very busy potential employers. The more you can give your agent to talk about, the better.

FYI: The givers of employment are impressed by people whose names keep popping up. It creates curiosity. It can generate momentum. Whatever your product is, keep it coming. If the initial appointments your agent scores for you are not for huge or amazing jobs, treat them as if they are anyway. Bring your best game every time.

Remember, having an agent is preferable, but you *can* work professionally without one. It is possible. Many people have done it. All you need are auditions. There are multiple ways to line them up, including simply submitting your photo to a casting director, attending an open call (that are frequently announced on websites like Backstage.com), or knowing someone who is personally involved in that particular production. Auditions can also arrive via directors, producers, or other actors who know your work, or through a manager or any individual who has access to the decision-makers or gatekeepers on a particular project.

In the end, your agent or manager works for you. I know it won't feel that way at first. But it's the truth. If you're going to start thinking of yourself as a professional, you need to start developing professional sensibilities. At its best, the representative-client relationship is a true partnership (hopefully a fun partnership!), but it's also a business, so there will be ups and downs.

If you are fortunate enough to land an agent or a manager early in your career, congratulations! That means they see something in you worth representing. Develop that talent. Make sure you can deliver when called upon.

Eleven points to refer to in looking for an agent:

1. Your life is going to be a balancing act for a while. You need to solicit agents' attention, but stay aware of the message you are sending. If all you do is tend bar and then mail pictures and resumes after work, sorry, but you are not sending out much of a signal. You've got to do some "creating" and send a loud, clear message that you are an active, interesting, entertaining artist on your way up!

2. Be patient. Finding a rep often takes time. Don't get mad. Or depressed. Just keep going. Focus on the "art" part. Keep sending up flares. The agent will emerge.

3. At the very beginning of your career, almost any agent who wants to rep you is good news. If, after a period of time, there are no appointments, then it's time to move on. How long you wait before making that decision is up to you.

4. Before accepting an appointment with an agent, check them out online. IMDB Pro (the professional side of the fan site IMDB.com) is a good place to start. It costs a little, but is a great resource that will allow you to find out who different agents' clients are and how often those clients are working. If you spot any red flags (like a guy who is working out of his home), take a friend with you to the appointment (especially if you are a woman).

5. If they decline to rep you, all that means is that they are the wrong rep for you. Move on.

6. If you sign with an agent, help them help you. Be sure to share any useful information. Do you speak foreign languages or do martial arts? Are you a great singer or a hilarious stand-up comic? That kind of info can really help.

7. Stay in touch, but don't police them or give attitude. Let them do their job.

8. Once you have an agent, you are no longer "aspiring." You're in the game. So play the game and keep getting better at it. When they send you out, be sure to represent them well. Be on time, professional, and prepared. Be original. Be precise. And be your fantastic self.

9. If you have a contract with an agent and decide to leave, you must call them and tell them so. That conversation is often awkward, but it's the classy thing to do, as opposed to doing it by voicemail or email. If you have been on their roster for a while and haven't made them any money, chances are they won't fight to keep you. If your contract hasn't actually expired yet, you might need to follow up with a brief letter formally stating that you are severing your business relationship.

10. Agents and managers tend to arrive after you have committed yourself to being a good actor who is active (in any way you can be) within your current community of fellow artists. When you are good and work hard, people notice.

11. And finally: *Don't forget to thank your reps for their efforts!* That's very important. You'd be shocked to know how often artists forget to do that.

No one cares what you want to do.
So you have to care more. People fail
in this business—talented people—
because they give up on the struggle.
Recognize that the struggle is part
of the work you need to do, and
persevere. If you are talented, and not
deluded about your talent, and you
refuse to give up, you will succeed.

—Paul, TV director and executive producer on several
hugely popular shows

10

A PARTICULAR COURAGE

———

Becoming Employable

When I was in acting school, Bill Esper forbade us to perform in shows while we were training. His position was that this was a delicate time in our development, and being involved in some tacky showcase could pollute our delicate psyches and derail all we had achieved. Like my fellow classmates, I dutifully nodded my head in solemn agreement, while making sure my copy of *Backstage* was crammed deeply into my backpack.

At that time *Backstage*, which is now a website that I often write columns for, was the weekly bible for aspiring actors (and it still is). It came out on Thursdays and contained info about all the open calls for Equity shows as well as casting notices for all the nonunion showcase productions happening around the city. The vast majority of these showcases paid zero unless you were a union member, and then they paid about a dollar.

Despite my teacher's warning, I auditioned for a lot of them and was finally cast in a showcase (aka nonpaying) production of a wonderfully weird play written back in the '60s. The show was being produced in a cool space on the top floor of a building in the west 70s that was much nicer than many of the threadbare joints downtown, where a roach might crawl across your shoe at any moment.

I was very excited, since the role was a great fit for me: a repressed, screwed-up teenager from a small town who, when he feels sexually pressured, attacks his young girlfriend. This already tragic event then results in the death of a homeless man who tries to rescue her. The play was very fragmented and strange but had all these great scenes for me and the actor who would play my girlfriend. The role wound up going to an odd young girl who had a lot of issues. Since I don't want to be a judgmental turd here, I'll just say that she was talented, but her massive insecurity created many, many problems, one of which was, she had a very hard time remembering her lines. Her defense was that she couldn't memorize dialogue without first uncovering the truth beneath the words. It sounded good, but as opening night got closer, it became clear that although she had unearthed a small mountain of truth, she had almost no knowledge of whose turn it was to talk. I was constantly having to help her out by improvising or paraphrasing my own lines to get things back on track. Occasionally, when she couldn't come up with one of her own lines, she'd say one of mine. The producers wanted to fire her, but I pled her case, saying I didn't want to start over with a new actor five days before opening. We staggered through a couple of previews in which she seemed to be doing a little better than usual. Then, on opening night, she cut through the middle of my big climactic monologue (which I'd worked very hard on) with a massive, blood-curdling scream; a scream that wasn't due until the following page of the script. The light board operator, not knowing what else do to, killed my light, and I was plunged into darkness midspeech. The actors in the final scene scrambled awkwardly into place, and the play went on without me. If I'd had an ax, I would have murdered her right there on the stage in front of everybody.

I refused to speak to or run lines with her for about a week, until one day I discovered her on the stairwell just outside the dressing rooms. This was where a lot of the cast hung out to get a little peace and quiet before the show. There she was, head in her hands, weeping like she'd lost her last friend. She looked so nuts that my anger melted, and I asked her what was wrong. Through her tears, she sputtered out that she had invited some casting director to come to the show, and apparently now he was coming.

"And?" I said incredulously. "That's good news, isn't it?"

"Is it?" she asked between sobs. "If he hates me, I'll never get another job. And if he likes me, he'll just put me in something else, and I'll have to go through this all over again!"

Part of me wanted to scream, "Get the hell out of here! Get out of this theatre, you lunatic, and surrender this role to someone who can at least say the words in the right order!"

But I didn't say that. Instead, I said, "I understand."

The sheer fun of creating art coexists with the fear of flopping. Wherever there is opportunity, there is the risk of failure. In short, this job is not for everybody.

Despite the fact that our scenes together were never the same two nights in a row, the show was actually pretty well received, and for a hot minute the producers bravely attempted to move it off-Broadway, which would have given me my Equity card. They were serious enough that they secretly brought in another, saner actress, with whom we rehearsed and performed a clandestine backer's audition for some moneyed investors from New Jersey—who, in the end, did not take the bait.

The new actor was fine, but she did not possess the same nutty quality the original gal had had in abundance. Yes, the original actor was insane, but she put out that bizarre energy that only the truly disturbed possess, and even though she never learned all the lines and made a ton of mistakes, she was actually better in the role, and I missed her. Sadly, about a week after the backer's audition, the crazy girl called me. She'd heard a rumor that the show was going forward without her. Not wanting to hurt her feelings, I made the mistake of lying and saying I knew nothing about it.

"It's okay," she said coldly. "I know why you don't like me."

Before I could respond, she hung up, and I never heard from her again. I assume that she moved on to another profession that suited her better. Given how strange she was, I'm not sure what that might have been, but maybe something where she could work with animals or some situation where there would be little judgment or few consequences.

Young artists face a big climb up a tall mountain. The trail is very slippery and not well marked, so there are going to be times when you lose your footing and slide down quite a bit farther than you thought you would. People frequently talk about how the job requires a thick skin. I'm not sure I agree. I actually believe just the opposite. Part of becoming good at this is "thinning" your skin to the point where people can virtually see through it. And that takes guts.

When young artists ask me how to get started, I usually shrug my shoulders and say, "Just start." Audition for anything you can. Do readings. Act in student films. Volunteer your services to any writer or director who needs help. Identify the places where they are doing the kind of work you want to do, and inch closer to that spot every day. Some of the productions you land in will be garbage. If that happens, shine that shit up to the best of your ability, and then move on. It may seem like not much is happening at this stage of the game, but you are slowly, gradually building something very important. And the thing you are building is not your resume.

Ready?

You cannot be a good artist without taking real risks. And you can't take real risks unless you have guts. And you will never have guts unless you possess (or quickly develop) a healthy ego.

Please note: There is a big difference between a "healthy" ego and a gigantic or tragically out-of-touch ego. A gigantic ego is not much fun for anybody—certainly not for the person who possesses it, and certainly not for the people who have to deal with it. A healthy ego is one that can withstand opinions. A healthy ego has confidence—because confidence emanates from a solid work ethic. A healthy ego assumes there will be a future beyond the immediate project. A healthy ego can recognize and graciously accept both positive attention and a little constructive criticism. Those with healthy egos don't allow detractors to dampen their dreams for long. A healthy ego doesn't have to beg for acceptance. A healthy ego gratefully assumes its rightful place and is a fast learner. An embarrassing defeat is not the end of the world; it's a challenge to be overcome. It's a mistake to be checked off the list. "Never have to trip over that again" is the motto of a healthy and adventurous ego.

Some people are born with this equipment already in place, and if you are one of those fortunate souls, may I say "Congratulations!" Others, like myself, start off with a slightly battered version and slowly trade up until we eventually find ourselves behind the wheel of a new, fully equipped model. This reward comes gradually through the craft of creating. Creating is, by its very nature, healing. It took a while, but in time I discovered I didn't need bravado, excuses, or false modesty to do my job, because I had an imagination. And the ability to use that gift gave me all the courage I needed. Everybody's journey is different, so if you require some help, get it. If you need a great teacher, they exist. If you need an artistic home, find it. If you need a terrific therapist, they're around.

In short: Whatever stands between you and your ability to believe you can do the work, overcome it.

Any creative career is a journey, and your journey begins with proving to the world (and more importantly, to yourself) that you can do it. My costar was derailed not by her nuttiness (there are a lot of nutty people who succeed) but by her massive insecurity, which kept her from believing she was capable of doing the job. Hence she squandered valuable time shooting herself in the foot.

Any decent artist must not be afraid to be seen. They must instinctively sense when their creation is worthy. And when that work takes flight, they understand how that liftoff was achieved. If you want that healthy ego, and the confidence that comes with it, do this: Pay attention. Stay awake. Be present. Don't kid yourself. Don't beg for praise or make excuses. Instead, notice how the world responds to you and your art, then use that information. Get good. Then get better. Most people struggle with prying open the door between what is and what could be. Kick the door down. Become interested. Prepare. Prioritize. Dwell in possibility. Answers are coming. Start recognizing them as they arrive.

When you actually know you can do the work, people will start noticing. And things will start changing fast.

Four thoughts before we move on to part two:

1. In the words of a long-dead Greek guy, "Know thyself."

2. In the words of David Dean Bottrell, "Know what thyself *is good at*—and get better at *that*."

3. In the words of one of Hawaii's greatest entertainers, Bette Midler: "The funny thing about this business is you have to believe you're the greatest thing since sliced bread, while also knowing you can always be better."

4. In the words of one of my former agents, "If they don't let you in the front door, you have to be the sort of person who will find the back door, or come through the window, or down the chimney! Whatever it takes, you have to believe you can do it, or you'll never get inside the clubhouse."

PART TWO

OPENING THE DOOR

Once you become a contender, new opportunities
will start to emerge.

And you'll meet someone interesting on this road: yourself.

**THE BEST THING ABOUT
SHOW BUSINESS?**
The waiting room at an audition.
That's where you see your fellow
artists, shake your head, and know
you are not alone in your love
for the craft.

**THE WORST THING ABOUT
SHOW BUSINESS?**
Having an audition in Santa Monica
at 3:30 p.m. to play a potato in an
Ore-Ida commercial when your agent
has you coming all the way from Los
Feliz where you just auditioned
to play a tomato in a pasta sauce
commercial.

—Kyle, TV and film actor and director

11

ROLE CALL

———

The Wonderful World of Auditions

When I was a young actor, as much as I loved acting, I loathed auditions. I was thrilled to be in a rehearsal hall, on stage, or in front of a camera, and I was obsessed with the whole process of discovering and crafting a character. But before I could hope to do that work I had to jump through these terrifying rings of fire know as auditions. I always walked into the room feeling like I was facing a firing squad, until (through a random stroke of fate) my perspective on auditions changed pretty radically.

The turning point came when I was offered a few bucks by a casting director to read with all the actors who were coming in to audition for a particular project he was casting. For the next few days, I got to watch the casting process up close and learn volumes about what to do (or not do) in the room. Since the casting director liked me, soon this one-time gig became sort of a recurring thing. Some actors were amazing. They were so comfortable you'd swear they were working in their living rooms. Others were so nervous that they accidentally came off as aloof or disinterested in the project. Some did stupid things like bring a ton of props with them to create their character's kitchen. I once saw an actor throw a full beer bottle against the wall. In case you're wondering, he didn't get the job, and I was the one who had to clean up the beer. But the most eye-opening education I got from this experience was listening to the wide range of opinions expressed about these performers by the directors, producers, and casting people after the actors had left.

Actors I'd thought were terrific were sometimes deemed too something for the role (too big, too small, too old, too young, too good-looking, not good-looking enough). The list went on and on. Occasionally, some actor who I thought had given a pretty flat and uninteresting reading would be praised for his subtlety and depth. Some actors were unanimously praised (while still in the room) for their skill and talent, but then disqualified after their exit by some odd technicality ("She's just too healthy-looking" or "He's a bit tall for this, isn't he?").

I began to realize that who got the role was not always determined by mere talent and sometimes came down to a matter of opinion. Instead of upsetting me, this knowledge began doing wonders for my mental health.

More than once, I had finished up an audition absolutely certain that I'd knocked their socks off, only to wind up waiting for a call that never came. I was now learning that I probably had knocked off at least a few socks, but so had the other guy (the guy who got the role). Obviously, they couldn't hire both of us. They had to pick somebody. It wasn't that I didn't have talent. It just wasn't my day.

When you're a young performer, those early jobs mean a lot. They are the desperately needed proof that you didn't make a huge mistake by spending all that money on acting school and headshots. Plus, like it or not, you are probably tracking the progress of your peers and feeling a little competitive with them. It's tough for new artists to keep their dream alive. When I teach audition workshops, I try to reassure everybody that trying to get the job is a terrible approach. My advice is to basically claim the role from the minute you walk in the door, zero in on the person who is reading with you, and then act the crap out of material. Pretend like it's opening night, or that the director just called "Action." Make something happen in the room.

Emboldened by what I'd witnessed as a "reader," I started sticking my neck out a bit more in auditions. I began to worry less about trying to second-guess what my potential employers might want and to instead focus on how to make this character I was auditioning for truly my own. Soon I started to book jobs that I hadn't expected to, because I simply took the time to look behind what the character was saying and tried to focus on how this character operated. What weird little detail from their history might be driving them?

A note of caution: Whatever you do to personalize and bring a character to life, make sure those choices are compatible with the material. If there's no indication in the script that your character has a Lithuanian accent or a limp, adding those kinds of extreme changes might not help your cause. In fact, they might make you look like a chump. As actors, we're there to serve the scene, not to hijack it and twist it into something it was never intended to be. The goal is to find an engine that drives the character and make sure you're *truly* doing what the character is doing in the scene (negotiating, seducing, undermining the other person).

Needless to say, I didn't book every job I went in for, but I was learning an important lesson: If I did well in an audition (even if I didn't book the job), it usually meant that I would be called back by that casting director to read for another job at some point in the future. Sometimes it would be a year or more before I got the call, but it usually happened. And often it represented the beginning of a long professional relationship with their office.

Soon auditions became less threatening and slowly morphed into just a part of my job. This represented a big change for me. In the past, I'd felt like I had to walk into every audition and prove to everybody that I was an utterly brilliant actor capable of playing every emotion in the rainbow during the four minutes I was in the room. I now enjoy auditions because I've come to realize *almost everything in the audition process is out of my control*. The only thing that is in my control is *my work*.

My work includes my talent, my ideas, and my knowledge of what this character is *actually attempting to do at this moment in his life*. It's not my job to trick anybody into hiring me. It's my job to (a) clearly "live" this moment as truthfully as possible, (b) be unafraid of the task, and (c) show them what only I can do with this material. It's that simple.

A few years ago, I was reading for a role of a man who was dissolving into madness, and the material was very emotionally charged. When I stepped into the room, I sensed that the casting directors were behind schedule. I took my position in front of the camera and began to give myself over to what I imagined it would be like to free-fall into unimaginable paranoia. Within a matter of seconds, I heard the casting director say, "We're rolling," with a tinge of impatience in her voice. In the old days, I probably would have been thrown, and started before I was ready, but instead I thought to myself, *Sorry gang, but I have a job to do here, and like it or not, I'm gonna take up four more seconds of everybody's time to do it well*. Approximately four seconds later, I looked up at the camera and exploded into the scene like a rocket. At the conclusion of the audition, everyone in the room was very nice to me. I booked the role and had a terrific time shooting the scene a few weeks later.

Every actor who expects to be hired has to radiate self-confidence in her or his own abilities. Personally, I don't want anyone in the room wondering if I can pull this off. If I'm standing in the audition room, I am pulling it off. The role is (at least for those few minutes) wholly and completely mine. Every audition is a chance to play a new character (which is, after all, why we're in this to begin with).

More and more actors are being asked to self-tape their auditions (for both TV and theatre) and then electronically submit those videotaped auditions to the casting director. If you are clueless about cameras and video-sharing services like Hightail.com or video storage sites like Vimeo.com, it's time to educate yourself a bit. If you're utterly intimidated, in most major markets there are now commercial companies that will handle the whole self-taping process for you at their office. All you have to do is show up. You can easily avoid that expense by shooting your self-taped auditions on a smartphone. If you want to use a fancier camera, feel free. Most casting directors will request that you "slate" at the beginning of the tape, which means you need to say your name (and sometimes your height) before you start your audition. If you want your self-taped audition to get noticed (in the positive sense), there are three things that you must pay attention to:

1. The tape must look good from a technical standpoint—meaning the camera is not shaking, you're well-lit, the sound quality is good, and the background is basically neutral.

2. You must be framed in a flattering, effective way. Sometimes moving the camera just two inches in one direction or the other can radically change how gorgeous or threatening you look. The best framing is usually from mid rib cage to the top of your head. You should be looking just to the left or right of the camera lens (not directly into it).

3. Most importantly, you need to give a kick-ass audition. That will be impossible if you don't have another human being just off-camera to work off of. Get one to work with you. Stand still. Listen. Focus on what your character wants. Do a bunch of takes. Submit the best one.

Only a scant few actors don't audition. The vast majority of us will be auditioning until the day we die or quit the business, whichever comes first. So instead of dreading auditions or being haunted by the jobs we don't book, it's important to make peace with the process and take pride in doing auditions well. There is no way to second-guess this process or what will happen. We can only do our work.

Many directors will tell you, "I don't know what I want until I see it." It's true. Having directed a few shows myself over the years, I can say that I often wound up casting actors who surprised me by bringing something to the party I hadn't expected: something larger or smaller, funny or poignant, clever or freaky, but something uniquely born of their own experience or imagination.

The eight-point audition checklist:

1. At the beginning, you'll have to get auditions on your own! Join the websites ActorsAccess.com and Backstage.com. Both will cost you some money, but are probably the best sites for the beginning actor. You'll then receive email alerts about auditions you might be right for. Even after you land an agent, you need to remain diligent in looking for work. It's your career, so stay on top of it.

2. Be prepared! Don't be lazy. Memorize the material. If you are genuinely pressed for time, then make sure you memorize the first page and you have a strong opening action to play. Let me repeat: *Always start strong!* This is especially true for taped auditions, where the directors are probably many miles away and all they will have to look at is this taped version of you. If you start strong, you will have directors' interest, and they will be more likely to forgive any minor flubs that occur on the second or third page of the material. In a perfect world there are no flubs, because no matter how busy you were, you made the time to fully prepare.

3. In every scene ever written, somebody wants something, and something goes wrong. Remember that! Learn to find those elements in the material and make sure they are present in your audition.

4. Listen. Be present in the room. If you're not listening, you won't be any good. Listening is like electricity. Actors who truly listen command attention.

5. Work off the reader. Usually, that person will not be an actor, so don't let that surprise you. Usually, it's an assistant who works in the office who is just trying to feed you your cues. Whoever the reader is, make sure you are working in response to their actual physical presence in the room. This is imperative for taped auditions. If you are talking around them, past them, or to the wall over their head, it will be painfully apparent. Acting is a human art form, and you have to be working off of another real human being for it to truly work.

6. Everyone has nerves. Try to keep in mind that nerves are just adrenaline, a natural substance your body generates when it senses it's time to run fast or jump high. Even famous people get nervous. It's not a mark of amateurism. Learn to channel that adrenaline into what your character wants. Use it to serve your goals.

7. If, after your audition, the casting director asks that you do it again with a suggested adjustment, realize that they are trying to help you. Do the adjustment as completely as you can. There is no time to rehearse this change or think it over for a day or two. The only thing to do is to jump off the cliff. Take the idea and run with it. Show them you are skilled and willing to take a chance.

8. Many actors ask a lot of questions about what to say or do in the audition room. My answer is simple. Enter the room politely. Do your work. Exit the room politely. The only definition of "politely" I can give you is to make sure that nobody in the room gets frightened or injured in any way. If you're hilarious by nature, go for it. If you're reserved, be that. Be yourself. Sometimes the job-givers will want to chat. Sometimes not. Whatever happens, strive not to be a jerk or come off as painfully desperate or dangerously insane. Whatever happens, do *your* part to make the audition process as comfortable as possible for all parties involved. The only thing that ultimately matters is the quality of your work. Leave them impressed by *that*.

The best thing about show business is when you win, you really win. There's no feeling on earth like it.

—Maya, actor and voice-over artist

12

LIFTOFF

———

The First Gig!

It was my first day as a professional actor, and I couldn't have been more excited. I had auditioned for and then been hired to act in a controversial British play being produced by a professional regional theatre company in Buffalo, New York. I had been working my butt off in acting school and had been granted an eight-week leave of absence to do this play. I had been in New York a little over two years, and things were finally happening.

Contract in hand, I had marched proudly down to the headquarters of the Actors Equity Association on West 46th Street so I could join the union. (More on unions in the next chapter.) Having never joined a union, I didn't realize that there was an initiation fee. Although by today's standards what they were asking wasn't much, at the time it was more than I had. Luckily, the nice lady in membership informed me that the fee could be taken out of my weekly salary using a payment plan. This was great news, since I had no idea how I was going to pay my rent that month.

I was flown to Buffalo (my third time on an airplane) and entered the rehearsal hall, where I quickly met all of my very jovial castmates. After some introductions and presentations by the designers, we sat down to read the play. I was particularly excited to hear it out loud since I'd already read it twice and did not understand a single word of it.

The play was a highly charged, multidimensional British political drama; part of it took place in present-day England, while other scenes took place in the early 1950s in Czechoslovakia, and bridging all of this was our leading man/narrator, who would step out of the action to deliver these long, complex monologues about political ideology. The show was very long, with a huge cast and a nonlinear plot that was sometimes challenging to follow. I played an angry seventeen-year-old Cockney lad who worked in a potato chip factory and was considered "disturbed" and slightly dangerous. The play consisted of a zillion short scenes, each one ending with something gross or upsetting. Clearly, the playwright was determined to get a rise out of the audience no matter what it took.

At the conclusion of the first read-through, there was some applause and lots of jokes (none of which I understood). I nodded my head a lot during the ensuing discussion of the play, but in truth, I was even more confused than I had been going in.

As rehearsals commenced, I worked very hard and conscientiously tried to educate myself. At the local library, I learned a little about communism, a little about the revolution in Czechoslovakia in the '50s, and, from a fellow cast member, that "crisps" were what they called potato chips in England. Then one day in rehearsal, I raised my hand and asked our very polite British director what the term "bugger" meant. I instantly sensed I'd made a big mistake, as a deafening silence fell over the rehearsal hall. He cleared his throat and, with all the dignity he could muster, gave me what sounded like the Oxford English Dictionary's definition of the term "buggery."

I could feel my face go hot as I blushed a deep shade of crimson. "Oh, okay," I replied. "That's what I thought."

On top of my ignorance of history, I was discovering that my role, which I'd been so excited about, was turning out to be really hard to pull off. Like many young actors, I wanted nothing more than to play distant, dangerous, misunderstood young men as brilliantly as James Dean or Marlon Brando had done in the '50s. But I was having some trouble drumming up the particular kind of rage my character possessed. At one point, I asked another young actor in the cast, Evan Handler, if I sucked. Evan, who was a classy guy even back then, said, "Well, no . . . you don't suck. But maybe you could relax a little."

He was being kind. I was a mess. Mostly because something was becoming very clear to me. To quote *The Wizard of Oz*, I wasn't in Kansas anymore. From the first read-through of the play, I'd been struck by the very clear fact that I was now working with professional actors with long resumes. Even the younger actors like

Evan had done a heck of a lot more than I had. I was used to being in showcases, school plays, or community theatre, where I'd always believed that I shone. This was a different ballgame. Here, everybody shone.

I was discovering the difference between my dream of being a professional and this very new reality.

In my dream, a job in show business would look like this: I land the part. Then we all laugh, fart around, crack each other up, have a lot of impromptu parties, and then, somehow, opening night arrives and I deliver a terrific performance followed by thunderous applause and critical accolades. I hadn't really thought much about what comes in between. I really hadn't realized the amount of work needed, or the complexities involved in creating an integrated, balanced, fluid performance. I had no idea how the sausage got made.

I took Evan's advice. I did relax a bit. I learned to channel my fear that I was talent-less into a seething anger that served me well during my more dramatic scenes. I don't think I was brilliant, and I certainly never approached Dean or Brando ter-ritory, but I acquitted myself decently. Although the reviews were respectful, the audiences of Buffalo, New York, utterly hated the play. And nobody could really blame them. One of their primary industries, Bethlehem Steel, had just closed its doors, and nobody was much in the mood to listen to a long-winded tirade about the virtues of communism. The audiences walked out in droves; on a good night we could expect to lose about a third of our ticket-buyers after intermission. In response, we formed a pool backstage where everybody pitched in two dollars and guessed the number of walkouts for the evening. The exact number would be verified by the house manager, and whoever came closest won the pot. Soon this got dull and the rules were adjusted so that you had to hit the exact number to win. One night I guessed it correctly and used my $252 to buy drinks for the cast and crew after the show.

About midway through the run, our leading man (who was married and a recover-ing alcoholic) started having a fling with one of the female cast members. He then fell off the wagon and started showing up drunk for performances. To his credit, he mostly remembered his lines, but he added seven minutes to the running time of an already long show.

So my first professional experience was neither a smashing success nor was it a disaster. It was a job in a show for which I was paid money. It got me into a union, plus gave me a start on some grown-up things like health insurance and an unem-ployment claim. It introduced me to a theatre company that would repeatedly employ me in the years to come. But most of all, it allowed me into a whole new world, populated by some very talented and hardworking artists. I had exited the bush leagues, and it was time to step up my game.

During the run, one of the other young actors in the show confided to me that this was also her first professional gig and that she had decided to leave the business after the show closed.

"I thought this would be more fun. I don't really like it."

I understood what she was saying, but I'd already caught the bug, and now I was hooked. I wanted to see how far I could go.

Dreams are wonderful. They are as light and airy as balloons. You can lie in bed at night and toss them endlessly up in the air. And if one them falls and hits you on the head, no damage is done. Once you enter the big leagues, things change.

Perhaps the greatest gift that came from my first professional experience was the discovery that a dream could actually morph into something absolutely real. And just a heads-up: If you choose to make a life in this profession, your dreams will continue to morph. My dream became my job, and soon it was my mission. That mission was to be good enough to merit a spot on the new team that would soon be forming to create the next piece of art coming down the line. I had gotten in the door; now the question was how far I could go.

Is this your mission?

Five pieces of good news/bad news:

1. The two greatest gifts of show business are collaboration and camaraderie. The sheer fun of making something out of nothing and getting to hang out with interesting, smart, funny people is what hooks most of us. However, once we turn pro we quickly learn that the recipe that creates a great community theatre show is not quite the same one that creates a Broadway smash. If you like just having a fun time on stage with your pals, you can do that anywhere without necessarily doing this professionally. To do this professionally is not always fun.

2. I somehow thought that once I landed my first job, the next one would follow pretty quickly. In my case, the next paying job didn't arrive for eighteen months. There is zero job stability. Zero. Think about that. Because that reality doesn't work for most people.

3. The day you become a professional, you are entering into a workforce *jammed* with some of the most talented, smart, good-looking people on the planet. They will be your competition until the day you die. So before you invest an enormous amount of time and money and move to a big, crazy city, think it over. There is something to be said for being a big fish in a smaller pond.

4. If this is your mission, you will know it pretty soon after the train leaves the station. You will inherently sense that a place has opened up for you in this community of artists that you'll now be working with (and, at times, competing with). If you *don't* sense that change, pay attention to that feeling.

5. When you cross over to the professional side, you'll start to become more aware of what works. What I mean is you'll begin to understand what works for you artistically, plus you will also start to grasp some of what you will need to do if you want to get paid for your ideas and creativity. I believe that if you are honest and courageous, you'll find that the artistic and the professional can often walk comfortably hand in hand.

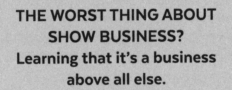

**THE WORST THING ABOUT
SHOW BUSINESS?**
**Learning that it's a business
above all else.**

—Victoria, TV writer, series creator, and showrunner

13

LABOR DAY

———

Joining the Union(s)

If you are already a professional actor, you can probably skip this chapter, but if you're in the starting gate, read on!

I still remember the day I got the news. I was sitting at my day job at a company that managed residential real estate in Manhattan, dutifully sorting through a huge pile of complaint forms from tenants who foolishly thought their rent entitled them to things like hot water or a front door that actually locked. My dreary day suddenly turned around when I received a call from Marla and Diane, informing me that I'd booked my first professional gig: the aforementioned British political drama. For a few seconds, I couldn't speak. Then I recovered enough to ask if I could call them back in ten minutes. I stared at the stack of complaints, then suddenly grabbed a handful and tossed them high in the air with a whoop of joy! Then, realizing what I'd just done, I quickly scrambled around the office picking them up before my boss saw the mess I'd made. After concocting a ridiculous story about needing to fill an emergency prescription, I fled the office and for the next few minutes skipped and danced through the streets of New York as if I were starring in my own private musical. It's hard to explain the feeling, but I actually thought I might choke to death on happiness. It seemed to be flowing up out of my twenty-two-year-old heart like a gusher. I stayed late at work that night to retype my resume (including my new credit), proudly adding the letters "AEA" under my name. I then photocopied about a million copies of it at the company's expense! I was finally a member of the Actors Equity Association!

One of the rites of passage for any professional actor is joining one or both of the unions: Actors Equity Association (AEA), which covers professional theatre performers, and SAG-AFTRA, which covers the majority of work done in front of a camera. Most New York actors belong to both. In L.A., you'll find a certain percentage of actors who belong only to SAG-AFTRA, since there are substantially fewer professional theatre opportunities on the West Coast than the East Coast. For a time, the Screen Actors Guild (SAG) and the American Federation of Television and Radio Artists (AFTRA) were separate unions until they chose to merge in 2012.

I've been a member of all these unions (plus the Writers Guild of America!) for some time now, and like many union members, at different points in my career I have had mixed feelings about how they were being run. Acting unions are governed by our fellow actors (and the hardworking nonactor staff), and they serve a large and somewhat moody membership who are not shy about expressing their opinions. Some of those opinions are well researched and worth hearing; others seem based on the premise that the unions are run by a legion of magical fairy godmothers who go around granting wishes. I have done a little service here and there for my unions, which has taught me a great deal about why and how things that should be simple to do quickly become complex. I've spoken on panels, volunteered at conventions, and marched in parades. I also walked the picket lines daily during the Writers Guild strike from November 2007 to February 2008 (sometimes in the rain!).

All in all, I'm a fan of my unions and avoid bad-mouthing them in public arenas. There is a school of thought that recommends young performers should avoid joining the unions and focus on nonunion work for the first few years of their career. I disagree. Joining as soon as you can will place you in the company of stronger, more accomplished artists, and working with them will automatically up your game. You will also gain more industry exposure and credibility as a professional.

Unions provide their members with safe working conditions, clearly defined work hours, job descriptions, a legal contract, and a firmly established salary. Other benefits include health insurance programs (based on your earnings), a pension plan, seminars, classes, referrals to social services, and a phone number to call if you encounter any kind of danger or abuse while on the job. SAG-AFTRA contracts provide residual payments for your work in the form of these wonderful checks that just magically appear in your mailbox, reimbursing you for the use of your work when it is rerun on network TV or cable or rebroadcast in foreign countries. The size of residual payments is determined by the kind of contract you were working on and how long ago you did the work. Sometimes the checks can be in the thousands; sometimes mere pennies. Whatever the amount, you are receiving that money because of your union, which continues to fight hard to keep those payments coming. Both SAG-AFTRA and Actors Equity have offices in both New York and L.A., plus regional offices around the country in areas where union employment is also available.

Most actors get union cards by being hired to perform in a union show. That means they managed to score an audition for a union gig and did well enough to book it. This audition could have arrived several different ways: (a) via their agent; (b) because they were invited to audition by the director or writer of the show, who was already familiar with their work; or (c) through the office of the casting director. (To reiterate, the casting director is hired by the producer to round up the best actors he or she can assemble to audition. Casting directors do not decide who gets the job; they only determine who will come in to audition. The director and producer must agree on which actors are ultimately hired. In most cases, casting directors will bring in new talent only if they are familiar with their work.)

There are other ways to join SAG-AFTRA and Actors Equity—through apprenticeship programs, by already being a member of the other smaller, lesser-known performing unions, or by doing a certain amount of background actor work (aka working as an extra). The best way to learn about those options is to check out the "How to Join" pages on the websites of SAG-AFTRA (www.sagaftra.org) and Actors Equity (www.actorsequity.org).

Be aware that all unions have initiation fees (to join) plus annual dues. And they are not cheap. All new SAG-AFTRA members pay a one-time-only initiation fee, plus the first semiannual dues at the time of joining. The national initiation fee rate is currently $3,000 (initiation fees may be lower in some regions outside New York and L.A.). Annual base dues are $214.32. In addition, work dues are calculated at 1.575 percent of covered earnings up to $500,000. Again, check the website for updates on all of this information.

Actors Equity Association currently has an initiation fee of $1,600 that must be paid within a maximum two-year period. Basic dues are $170 annually, billed at $85 twice a year. Working dues are currently 2.375 percent of gross earnings under an Equity contract, which is collected through weekly payroll deductions.

The maximum Equity earnings subject to working dues are $300,000 per year. Again, check the website for updates on all of this information.

Sometimes, when I get my biannual bill for union dues, I bristle a bit. Sometimes I think grumpy thoughts about how hard it is to make a living, and what are they doing except billing me for dues? But then I remember that they are doing everything they possibly can to better the lives of actors, and if I don't like what's happening, I should go run for a position on one of the national or local boards or volunteer for one of the many committees. Unions are complex living matrices with a lot of personalities, procedures, and agendas that must be navigated through or around. The biggest stars in our industry belong to the unions. Lesser-known, hardworking artists also belong. Geniuses belong. The nutcases belong. And very soon, you will probably belong. We're all in the same boat. The boat has a few leaks, but it's still afloat, and before 1919 there was no boat, and when nonfamous actors died, they were buried in unmarked graves in a potter's field. Unions have, without question, made things better for actors in general, and they have the potential to continue improving things in the future if we all remain actively involved. My suggestion: Stay aware of and involved in your union. Grab an oar and start rowing toward your future. Welcome aboard.

Five things to know about SAG-AFTRA and Actors Equity Association:

1. To work professionally as an actor, you must belong to one or both of them.

2. They cost money. Both charge initiation fees, and once you are in, they charge biannual dues.

3. Their memberships are huge. SAG-AFTRA had 116,741 ("active" members) as of 2016. Actors Equity Association had 43,648 as of 2015. Only a small percentage of those members actually make their living as actors.

4. The unions do their best to help their members navigate the industry, but they do not guarantee their members work. They do not produce work. They offer you protections and certain benefits *while* you are working.

5. Unions are only as good as their contracts, which are periodically renegotiated. I urge you to stay aware of any issues on the table. Again, consider becoming active in your union in some way. It is an investment in your future.

**THE BEST THING ABOUT
SHOW BUSINESS?**
**The feeling of gratification in
those moments when you realize
you're being paid to do what you
absolutely love.**

**THE WORST THING ABOUT
SHOW BUSINESS?**
**Having to constantly remind
yourself that your value as a person
isn't based on how work is going.**

—Victor, TV writer, producer, and sketch comedy performer

14

THE DISCOVERY CHANNEL

———

Who Exactly Are You?

Everybody starts out with a few heroes. When I was a young actor, I idolized Sean Penn. He was just so good, and although he was not traditionally handsome, he had enormous appeal and seemed to be the heir apparent to De Niro. He was a real artist with a dark, edgy sensibility, yet he had a core that was sensitive and easily injured. And he wore it all on his sleeve in a dangerous, yet moving kind of way.

Throughout acting class, I did my best to cultivate my best Penn persona. I smoked. I wore the most ragged clothing I could find, with big, clunky, beaten-up boots I'd gotten from a thrift store. I managed to use every exercise in my acting class to express some form of pent-up rage. My first professional role was sort of a Cockney Sean Penn part, and it proved to be a bit of a challenge for me.

The biggest problem was that I wasn't in any way like Sean Penn. My natural persona was high-strung, not reserved. I was talkative, not brooding. I was funny, not deep. My natural setting was happy, which was not the sort of misunderstood, "damaged goods" energy that young Mr. Penn exuded in those days.

I began to feel very, very sad. Fearing that I was a talentless nobody, I fought even harder to define myself as the next brooding superstar. I even got cast in another "Sean Penn" role. Granted, it was being produced in a church basement for no money, but I was excited. The play was Thomas Babe's *A Prayer for My Daughter*, and the role was a young junkie who may or may not have committed a murder.

It was a great part that really allowed me to chew the scenery, and I even got to take all my clothes off! (I was then twenty-three years old and, as I've said, extremely skinny.) The play took place in a police station and had a long, complex scene where I was being interrogated by a tough cop. I was so psyched! That is, until we started rehearsal—and once again I began to feel like I had conned these people into casting me. Everything I was doing felt forced and inorganic. I was a hack, a phony. But I kept showing up and soldiering on, praying that the spirit of Sean would come to the rescue.

Then one day when I was rehearsing my lines in my apartment I had an idea. I began to think about what a mess this guy was. I mean, he had just shot heroin, for God's sake. And I began to think about what that might feel like. I'd never been a junkie, but I'd been high and drunk enough times in my young life to understand how those things can instill a totally false sense of confidence in a person. I began to play with the idea of how this guy might suddenly be struck with the delusion that he had some power in this situation—when, of course, he had none. Long story short, my character's newfound bravado suddenly seemed so absurd, it felt funny. I could barely say the lines without cracking myself up. I took that choice into rehearsal that night, and everybody loved it. What had been a less-than-successful "tortured" character was now suddenly just a dumb kid, comically clueless and out of step with reality, dependent on a small amount of brains and a large amount of drugs to get him through life.

The most important thing I discovered was the importance of using what you have. All of the qualities I was trying to hide about myself (my humor, my energy, my desperation to win at a difficult game) were the very things I was now using to make this character into a living, breathing person. The show's short run soon became a word-of-mouth, sold-out hit, and the interrogation scene always got huge, unexpected laughs from the audience. The character's stupidity also gave him a real poignancy in the final scenes of the play. Although not seen by that many people, it remains to this day one of the best things I've ever done.

Not long after, I got a call. A famous young actor had dropped out of a very funny, balls-to-the-wall, one-act comedy called The Job Search, and they needed a replacement fast. The show was part of a high-profile one-act play festival being produced by the Manhattan Punch Line (a hot theatre at the time). Although only twenty-two minutes long, the play was hilarious and hugely challenging. I never left the stage and had to shift gears at lightning speed, as I and another actor played a rapid succession of scenes without so much as a chance to breathe between transitions. It was the most technically difficult role I'd ever done, and in no time

I'd completely run through my existing bag of comedic tricks. Having nothing else to make use of, I started to use myself. Meaning I found myself doing things on stage that I'd never done before. I was allowing myself to be seen as the desperate, clueless nerd that (until that moment) I'd only ever allowed my roommate to see. I was genuinely revealing myself and getting some very big laughs in the process. And the big surprise was how easy it was to do. Surely this kind of acting couldn't be any good. Still clinging to my unrequited love of Sean Penn's career, I kept thinking that good acting had to be sort of tortured, dark, and a little insane.

When the play was reviewed, my cohort and I got our names and faces in the *New York Times* with a very nice mention about our work. As a result, I signed with my first real agent. I couldn't believe it. What a shock! Apparently, struggling to imitate the success of another actor wasn't going to work. But using my hidden, totally taken-for-granted human qualities (and pushing myself to reveal as many of them as I could) was going to give me a career. I was not going to be the next Sean Penn, after all. I was going to be me.

I say this because many, many people I know stumbled onto their careers—meaning they stumbled onto some self-knowledge that gave them the keys to a door that previously seemed to be locked. Half the time, we don't know what we can do until we do it. Many artists' careers take off (or are substantially rejuvenated) when they take a stab at a genre, character type, or style of material they'd never really considered before. There is no real formula for this. It's mostly trial and error. But especially at the beginning of your career, be prepared for some surprises. You may not know who you are yet.

This stage of everybody's career is about discovery. When we set out on this journey, we have, at best, a tattered map left behind by a previous explorer. Although it may indicate the location of the ocean and a few major landmasses, it doesn't indicate which ports are still open and which unknown harbors may be revealed at any second. The history of show business is filled with people who came to town with one plan and found themselves with an utterly unexpected career. More than once, those who planned to be an innovator of modern drama wound up making people laugh on a sitcom. Believe me, almost anything can happen.

As you begin to become a professional, you're going to begin to discover yourself. Or at least aspects of yourself. And the business is going to discover you as well. Some job-giver is going to spot something they like about you, and that'll be the first door to open. It might be how you look. Your ability to improvise or tell a great joke. Your ability to scare everybody in the room. Your ability to cry on cue. Could be anything.

You cannot predict how or when these discoveries will happen. Whenever they occur, embrace them. Try them on for size. Sometimes they might seem random, but there's a secret logic to them. Wearing a different hat can be incredibly fun! Go for it.

The good news, delivered in five nautical metaphors:

1. Any small success in this business is a big deal when you think about the number of people who would kill for it. If you can get your ship into port *anywhere*, you've won. You're a winner.

2. If you sincerely think about it, there's probably a very real reason your ship docked where it did. That's not to say you can't sail elsewhere, but do not fail to recognize that you were entrusted with this gig by someone who had plenty of candidates to choose from.

3. The fact that you were even allowed into harbor means something all by itself. It was your talent that got you there.

4. Savor the victory, dazzle everybody, cash the check, and start charting your course for the next port. Never complain about not getting what you wanted. You actually did.

5. Drifting off course might be the best thing that could happen. Abandon nothing. Acknowledge everything. And build on what you've got.

An Oscar-winning actor once told me, "Don't worry about making money on the way up; you'll make plenty on the way down."

—Skip, veteran stage actor and director

15

UP IN MY BUSINESS

———

Paying the Bills

Between mentoring, the film festival circuit, and my gym, I've recently started making friends with a whole new group of actors and writers, most of whom are in their twenties. Many have what we in the business refer to as "money jobs"—the jobs that sustain us when we are first trying to get a foothold in the business or when we're between gigs. I'm very grateful that I haven't had to have one of those jobs in a while, but back in the day, I had plenty.

When I was a young unemployed college dropout living in Austin, Texas, I harbored big dreams of moving to New York to study acting but hadn't quite sucked up the guts (or the money) to do so. Finally, I registered with a temp agency and was sent to work in a large mailroom that handled all the mail for every social service agency in the state of Texas. There were about thirty-five of us in the mail-sorting room, many of us temps. It wasn't particularly challenging work, since every piece of mail had a numerical code printed on it, and you simply shoved the envelopes into the box with the corresponding number. The only tough part was lifting the heavy bins full of mail—and of course, the sheer monotony.

Our supervisor, Mr. Ramirez, was a kind, soft-spoken guy who appeared about twice a day to handle all the problems and complaints (of which there were many). But everybody who worked there knew full well that Mr. Ramirez didn't really run the mailroom. The mail-room was truly run by a thirteen-year veteran employee named Mabel-Ann.

Mabel-Ann was a fiftyish, tough-as-nails African-American woman who knew her job (and everyone else's) backward and forward. Because of the high employee turnover, she generally waited until you had been there at least three weeks before she bothered to learn your name. Mabel-Ann was a woman with many opinions, all of which she shared freely as she jammed the mail into mostly the right boxes. In fact, it was almost impossible *not* to know what was on Mabel-Ann's mind on any given day. Her constant chatter sort of annoyed me, but I did love it when some regional office would call to complain about their shredded mail, and Mabel-Ann happened to pick up the phone. She had a masterful way of dealing with such people; a way that, while staying within the guidelines of the employee handbook, also clearly conveyed to the caller that she didn't give a crap about them or their mail. She could be hilariously funny, but also surprisingly mean—especially if she felt threatened. One day, a temp worker innocently made a suggestion to Mabel-Ann about how she was handling the mail and received a blistering warning to "Never, not now, not ever, get up in my business again." And God help anybody who left a mess in the break room, because that "nasty-ass, sorry behavior" would work its way into Mabel-Ann's unending monologues for weeks to come.

I managed to avoid her for a while, but the mailroom was Mabel-Ann's fiefdom, so it was inevitable our paths would cross. And cross they did, one day during "Crunch." "Crunch" occurred every day at exactly 4:00 p.m. when (I kid you not) a loud buzzer would sound that sent us all scurrying like rats. The buzzer meant that all the mail had to be pulled, packaged, and loaded onto an outgoing truck in one short hour. It was a huge job. Whatever you were doing, you dropped it and rushed to the rows of mailboxes that lined the room. Beneath each box was a slot that contained a large manila envelope. Your job was to cram all the mail into this envelope, label it, seal it using your tape gun, and then toss it into the big cart that was hopefully behind you.

One day, as I was diligently trying to wedge a huge stack of mail into its corresponding envelope, I looked up to find Mabel-Ann glaring impatiently at me.

"We ain't got all day!" she barked. "Do it like this!" Grabbing the manila envelope from me with her left hand, she snapped it in the air, instantly cracking it open. Simultaneously, her right hand shot into the next mailbox and, with the strength she'd gained from thirteen years of doing this work, crushed all the mail into sort of an oblong wad and hammered it into the open envelope. Slamming it onto the counter, she slapped a crooked label on it, sealed it with a wrinkled piece of tape, and tossed it into the cart, where it banged roughly against the side.

Glancing at my horrified expression, Mabel-Ann huffed at me, "We ain't sending these to our mamas!" and marched away.

At the time, I didn't have the balls to point out that Mabel-Ann had just jammed the mail intended for the Fredericksburg office into an envelope bound for Freeport.

During the six weeks that I worked in the mailroom, I did manage to pick up a little more speed during "Crunch." I even became well liked enough to be the butt of a few of Mabel-Ann's jokes (which, believe me, was a good thing).

Mabel-Ann was the first real "star" I had ever dealt with. Like all stars, she had a big ego, and I quickly learned that it was well worth my time to say something engaging to her first thing in the morning. When I started bringing my lunch, I got invited to sit at her table in the break room, where I soon learned about her hardscrabble childhood, her shiftless ex-husbands, and her three grown daughters, none of whom had yet produced a single damn grandbaby. In time, I also learned about her dyslexia and diabetes, both of which she felt had kept her from her rightful place behind Mr. Ramirez's desk. I came to admire how Mabel-Ann had found ways of taking what was at best a crappy job and turning it into a reasonably entertaining way of spending your day.

One day I sprained my hand trying to crush a state resource directory into an envelope, and I knew it was time to resign my position in the mailroom. When I came in to get my final time sheet signed, Mabel-Ann hugged me and made a point of telling me I'd done a fine job.

Today, I'm sure that many of my new young friends tend to think of their money jobs as some sort of awful interruption of their lives, a huge pain in the butt that does nothing but rob them of what must seem like extremely precious time. I can understand this impatience, but money jobs serve two purposes.

The first is to pay our bills and allow us to pay for rent, classes, headshots, phones, tablets, and whatever else we need to further our careers. But they serve another unexpected purpose. They allow us to do a little living. And living (as it turns out) is not just complaining while we wait for better things to happen. Living is sometimes getting through the shift (an experience that much of the human race has every day). Work allows us to slowly learn the measure and cost of our choices. It builds strength and deepens the well. And most importantly, it makes us better students of the human animal.

As you might have already noticed, most scripted stories are not about the lives of famous, enlightened artists. They are usually about people working with somewhat less grandiose dreams.

During the time I was working in the mailroom, I couldn't have possibly predicted how many times Mabel-Ann's voice would, in the years to come, ring through my head as I sat writing African-American characters in screenplays for major movie studios (more on that saga later). When I was called in to audition for an important role on a very popular TV show, I summoned up a memory of an odd, wealthy man who used to hire me to bartend for him at private parties at his townhouse in the stylish Murray Hill section of Manhattan. He was genuinely insane, and I'm pretty certain that mimicking his imperious Yankee attitude and East Haddam accent were what got me the job that changed my entire career. The time I logged in the food service industry, or being a messenger, a housecleaner, and a telephone salesperson taught me a great deal about how people from backgrounds vastly different from my own navigated their lives.

Of course, nobody wants to stay in their money job forever, and I do advocate changing gigs occasionally, so that you (a) don't lose your mind and (b) allow yourself to meet yet more interesting citizens of the world. Sometimes these gigs can be a little painful and hard on our pride, but you should never discount the value offered to you by the inconvenient stretches of life. They are worth more than you think they are. Those bad bosses, irritating coworkers, or not-so-nice customers may someday pop up in your "business" at a very crucial moment, and you will be surprisingly grateful for the brief time you shared with them. It's often from life's unruly fabric that we stitch together our best, funniest, and most truthful work.

Seven things to keep in mind about money jobs:

1. The goal of a "money job" is to make money. Steer toward gigs where you'll make the most in the least amount of time. But don't do anything illegal.

2. Remember that these jobs must serve your needs. If they are preventing you from going to auditions or taking classes, you need to find a new situation. Think practically. If need be, think outside the box.

3. Some artists I know have discovered that they possess an entrepreneurial streak and have created businesses for themselves. While I applaud that idea, make sure it serves you. Creating a business means running a business. And that takes time. Sometimes a lot of time. Keep an eye on how your time is being spent.

4. The most common jobs that aspiring artists use to pay the bills are the ones that offer a flexible schedule. Some examples include waiting tables, delivering food, bartending, catering, substitute teaching (if you hold a degree), tutoring, nannying, dog walking, office temp work, house painting, and housecleaning. Keep in mind that there are many ways to make money, and don't be shy about asking your fellow artists how they are making ends meet.

5. If you happen to stumble onto a job that you really, truly love, pay attention to that. The universe might be sending you a strong message. Never ignore strong messages.

6. Although you might be firmly focused on being a "legit actor," there are opportunities to make money doing commercials, voice-overs, and print work. These areas (assuming you have a knack for them) can sometimes be very lucrative. Working as a background actor (aka extra work) is not glamorous, but it definitely puts you close to the action and can be very educational. Never miss chances to work within the industry.

7. Occasionally, money jobs can provide a genuinely unexpected or bizarre human experience that you will be able to treasure, cringe over, or laugh about in the years to come.

I ASKED A FEW FRIENDS: WHAT WERE SOME OF THE JOBS YOU DID TO PAY THE BILLS?

I was in sales for mulch at Lowes in Torrance, California. Terrible job and even more terrible city.

—Rachel, stage and TV actor

I was a telephone salesperson, selling lightbulbs to maintenance workers at schools and churches. I quit after one day.

—Frank, veteran character actor

Handing out samples of Honey Nut Clusters cereal at the Third Street Promenade in Santa Monica. We had to wear baseball caps with giant stuffed squirrels glued on top.

—Gabrielle, actor, comedian, and sketch performer

Overnight shifts of commercial painting; working for rich, racist aristocrats; nannying; delivering food during winter to the "trust funds" in Chelsea—that was the worst of them all.

—Taz, up-and-coming young actor and recent drama school grad

Dressing up as a Cabbage Patch Blueberry doll and talking in a southern accent, while giving away boxes of breakfast cereal on street corners in downtown L.A. and on the Venice Beach Boardwalk. Next was waitressing at Beefsteak Charlie's, where the customers could get all the beer, wine, and sangria they could drink with a salad bar.

—Christine, TV and stage actor and respected acting teacher

I was a cocktail waitress at the Snow White diner, then located at Columbus Circle. It was an "open twenty-four hours a day" diner. I was on the 12:00 a.m. until 8:00 a.m. shift. I wanted to leave my days open for auditions and classes. I ended up making a lot of drinks to go.

—Roz, popular theatre, TV, and film actor

I was temping for a hedge fund as a front desk assistant. My job was to answer phones for the boss, but being that I couldn't even pronounce his name correctly, I was let go after lunch.

—Parker, TV and film actor

Working a trade show for a dragon lady. Twelve-hour days. On my feet the whole time. No breaks. Fun.

—Talia, TV and film character actor

I worked the graveyard shift at a bagel shop/convenience store under the train in Staten Island. Constant stream of prostitutes and drug dealers. Made $6.00 an hour under the table but could eat all I wanted. Had to clean rat traps as the sun rose.

—Xavier, actor, playwright, and screenwriter

My worst job was being a chef at a local bowling alley in New Jersey. On the bright side, I can make a delicious quesadilla!

—Sarah, up-and-coming young actor and recent drama school grad

Filling in for receptionist. Left everyone on hold. And couldn't really type well.

—Adrienne, veteran screenwriter

I delivered sandwiches for Between The Bread to yuppie corporate scum.

—Toby, theatre and TV actor

Receptionist at a furniture store. I just stared out the window.

—Luciana, TV and film character actor

Assistant to a business manager who called himself a producer, even though he was simply a business manager.

—Vanessa, TV writer, show creator, and showrunner

The worst job I had was proofreading US government Occupational Safety and Health Administration (OSHA) manuals. I corrected spelling mistakes in what seemed like never-ending documents. I compensated by drinking wine while proofing.

—Ivan, well-known comic actor, writer, and producer

Emceeing a Jell-O wrestling event in a Wall Street bar.

—Zachary, TV, film, and stage actor

Worked twenty years in the corporate world as a credit manager, doing acting part-time. I never took vacations, so I could take time off if I booked a job, which I did! Then one day during a meeting, I politely told my new boss that he didn't have all the figures and that we would be bankrupt in six months if we didn't address certain issues. He asked to see me after the meeting and said, "You are a woman. No more than a goat. Don't ever contradict me again." Needless to say, I quit, and they went bankrupt in three months! And I have an Emmy!

—Paulina, TV and film actor; credits include a long stint on daytime drama

Show business is like the insane asylum. Anyone can apply, but only the truly insane are admitted.

—Anonymous

16

CRAZY IS AS CRAZY DOES

―――――

Working with Interesting People

The entertainment industry is mostly populated by talented, sane, and hardworking people. But there are certainly moments when you have to wonder who left the door open, allowing a surprising number of horribly behaving people into the clubhouse. I'm not talking about the jolly eccentrics—the quirky artists who get on your nerves but ultimately deliver when the chips are down. I'm referring to those nightmarish, dreadful people who gum up the works, overturn the boat, hog all the oxygen, and stink up the joint. Sadly, I can think of several such people without even trying very hard. Sometimes these individuals can amazingly float along for years based on one lucky break. As any of us who have ever been forced to work with one of these folks can attest, things can quickly go from "difficult" to surreal.

Early in my career, I did a revival of a not-so-great play from the 1950s with a "celebrity" whose only claim to fame was her role in an infamous sex scandal that had brought down a popular public figure. Despite having no acting experience whatsoever, she got herself into a prestigious class taught by a very famous (and very elderly) acting teacher who christened her an undiscovered genius. Buoyed by this endorsement, she then snagged herself a wealthy boyfriend and somehow conned him into financing her off-Broadway debut. I joined the production about a week before it opened, replacing an actor who had wisely chosen to bail. By this point, the play had notoriously gone through three directors and several cast changes, mostly due to the coarse and violent behavior of our star, who could easily have been mistaken for one of the hookers working on nearby 10th Avenue.

The show (which was a horrible train wreck) mercifully closed after about two performances, but during that brief time I witnessed three historic meltdowns, the last of which occurred on opening night when our star locked herself in her dressing room, claiming that one of us was trying to murder her. When she didn't show up the following night for the performance, no one knew what to do. Her understudy had already quit, and we had seven people sitting in the audience (six of whom were the leading man's relatives who'd all driven in together from New Jersey).

Suddenly, the backstage pay phone rang. Curious, I answered. It was our star, informing us she didn't feel like doing the show and to vacate the premises immediately. When the leading man grabbed the receiver to demand that she show up and perform for his family, things got ugly fast. Soon vile, disgusting names were being screamed back and forth until our leading man finished with a really fancy one before slamming down the receiver. Two seconds later, the phone rang again, but this time a shy, mild-mannered character actress shrieked, grabbed the receiver, and let loose with an even more shockingly accurate insult before hanging up on our star. This pattern was repeated a couple more times as the last remaining cast members lined up to vent a few feelings that had been building up over the past few weeks. When the phone rang for a final time, I was the only person left.

Our star's first question was, which cocksucker was she talking to now?

"It's David," I replied. "The new guy."

"Oh," she said, sounding a little disappointed. She then informed me that I was to deliver several disgusting messages to various cast members.

"Okay," I said quietly.

"I know you won't do it," she replied. "You're too nice. But you tell those motherf**kers they better get their chickenshit asses out of that theatre or I'll have them all arrested for trespassing! I'm calling the cops now!"

When I reported to my castmates that we were all about to be arrested, the company agreed that that would be the perfect way to bring this show to an end. Gathering our belongings, we waited in the lobby for a while, drinking wine with the leading man's family. But sadly, the cops never came. Finally, we all hugged and went home. The show was over—in every sense of that phrase.

Sometimes, even talented people become unhinged when they are out of their element. Drowning in self-doubt, they can begin to think of themselves as a castle under siege. Suddenly, you are either "with them" or "against them," with no middle ground. A few years ago, a friend of mine was cast in a sitcom that featured a well-known stand-up comic in the lead. When I asked him how things were going, he sighed and said it was a basically easy gig. He explained that each week the show started out with a fairly normal script, one that included a serviceable plot, with lots of jokes spread out evenly among the characters. But gradually in the course of rehearsals the star would whine and scream and weep and threaten everyone until all the funny lines were eventually handed over. By the end of each week, my friend's contribution to the show basically amounted to sitting on the sofa and saying some version of, "You're kidding! So then what happened?"

"On the plus side," my friend added, "my lines aren't hard to memorize, since they're the same ones I said last week."

Before I became a professional, I had never witnessed anything like this. I had assumed that when the big shift came, and we were all working for actual money, everyone's behavior would naturally skyrocket to the highest possible standard. And for the most part, that's been true. But occasionally you will find yourself working with a kamikaze pilot determined to ruin everybody's good time. I wish I could tell you what the right course of action is, but in the end, it's sort of a personal call. Once or twice, I have managed to charm a couple of these individuals into behaving a little better so we could get through the experience. But in a couple of cases, I've had to lock horns and let things get genuinely unpleasant, because anything less would have been a complete surrender to crappy behavior.

In the end, I try to think of the welfare of the show itself. The one thing that everybody in this business needs is a job—meaning a project that is going forward. When some asshole threatens to stall or utterly derail things, I believe that my first loyalty is to the people who have hired me. When someone implodes, everybody's goal should be to get the project through to the finish line, whatever it takes. Fortunately for me, I'm generally pretty patient—well, most of the time. Yes, I've screamed into a couple of phones, sent a few not-so-smart emails, and burned a bridge or two, but honestly, those instances have been rare. Mostly, I've gotten a lot of praise for keeping it together and have been rehired by a couple of directors for biting my tongue and hammering through.

Years ago, I found myself in a play with a really difficult scene to perform opposite someone who was kind of an argumentative ass. He couldn't get through five lines of dialogue without picking a fight with somebody, and he wasn't very good in the role. Although I was managing to keep my mouth shut, I was truly starting to hate him. I went to my teacher, Bill Esper, for help, and he gave me some fantastic advice: "You cannot play drama critic and act at the same time. Whoever this guy is, you have to take the position that he is brilliant. He's the most amazing actor since De Niro. You have to work off of him like he's the second coming. It's the only way to free yourself." And he was totally right. That advice saved my neck. When I applied it, the actor settled down and started connecting with me. On some level, he began picking up that I was now giving him my complete respect, and he rose to the occasion. His work improved dramatically, and believe it or not, that scene became one of the highlights of the show.

I have no idea what causes people who are fortunate enough to be employed in my industry to behave badly. I suppose it's the pressure, or inexperience, or addiction issues, or maybe some hidden crap that predates their entry into the business. Who knows? This is a stressful industry, and when you are the star (or think you are) that stress gets worse. I've had people ask me why show business seems to attract such a dependable percentage of wackos. I'm not sure, but I sometimes wonder if they arrive that way or it's the business itself that makes them turn the corner. The self-imposed pressure to be the hippest, smartest, most talented artist on two legs seems to always be hovering over our shoulder. And maybe that's not so bad in the end. It keeps us thinking and pushing for more.

So here's the good/bad news: if you're not a little nuts coming in the door, you probably will be soon. Just try not to let it rule the day.

And one final little piece of sad truth (I can't believe I'm saying this): Having a little bad behavior rain down can sometimes be a good thing. More than once, I've seen the work improve because the boat got rocked a bit. It might piss us off, but it also keeps us on our toes. It gives us a good story to tell and reminds us that a little lunacy, although inconvenient, will always keep the proceedings interesting and genuinely charged. If you haven't seen it yet, you will.

Five rules for dealing with bad behavior:

1. First off, let's be clear about this: it is a new day in the workplace. If you are the target of any form of sexual harassment, physical or verbal abuse, or bullying, speak up. Blow the whistle loud and long to whomever is in charge. Make it clear that if the behavior isn't addressed immediately, you'll take the issue upstairs or to the press. Protect yourself. However, if the bad behavior is not sexual in nature or directly abusive, here's my suggestion . . .

2. If the person who's behaving badly (selfishly, rudely, aggressively) is the star or the boss, do your best not to engage. Take a deep breath and try to work around them.

3. Even if the troublemaker is *not* the star or your boss, try to keep your feelings to yourself. Offer the individual as much cooperation as you can. You're not in their shoes, so it's impossible to truly know where this is coming from. Sometimes, if you are supportive, they will calm down and things will improve.

4. If you are confronted with a nutcase or a monster and you have a solid relationship with the director or producer, discreetly plead your case, but never say it's impossible to work with this person. If the person is the star, that comment might get you released from your contract. Align yourself with the good guys and try to get through the experience. It's a drag, but it won't last forever, and as I mentioned before, it will turn into a good story. Plus, you will grow as an artist and as a human being by going through it.

5. Once again, if the problem is sexual harassment or physical or verbal abuse, don't be polite or patient about it. Call it out. Such behavior is no longer acceptable. Period.

I started in New York, wanting to be a stage actor. I still am, but honestly, I regret not being bold and heading to L.A. when I was younger to at least give that location a chance.

—Lily, stage and TV actor

17

HAPPY MEDIUM

———

The Difference Between Stage and Screen

For most of my twenties, I worked the road. An old friend of mine from my Austin days, Nick Wilkinson, had become a casting director and cast a lot of regional theatre shows up and down the East Coast. He thought I was good, and happily I was able to book quite a bit of work through his office. The gigs were with resident professional theatres that paid a decent if not a princely wage. For about six months out of every year, I was usually out of town, living out of a suitcase while making a little art on some regional stage, usually located in the slightly dodgy downtown arts district of a large northeastern city. The jobs were always fun, and I can honestly say that this period of my life taught me not only how to be an actor but also, more importantly, how to be a trouper.

Unlike on-camera work, theatre is truly the actor's medium. While TV and film performances are largely crafted in the editing room, theatre places that responsibility entirely in the hands of the actor. It's also your job to lead the audience through the story you are telling. And probably the greatest joy and challenge of that job is to walk out on that stage each night and get acquainted with the ticket-buyers you're going to be working with. Sometimes they are attentive and utterly with you. Sometimes they are restless and bored, drop their programs, and cough a lot. Because theatre can never compete with TV and film when it comes to salary, stage work largely remains a labor of love. I spent my young adulthood on stage, and I'll always be grateful for all the amazing things I learned and experienced as a result.

Because I was primarily working in regional theatre during that time, I . . .

- Savored the incredible opportunity to actually act for two or three hours a night, six nights a week.

- Worked with a new live audience every night.

- Learned to play a dulcimer and a xylophone, and sing (out loud by myself).

- Discovered that I could pull off a passable minuet, although my true forte was the more "peasanty" folk dances.

- Played Shakespeare, Beckett, Euripides, Kaufman and Hart, and Lillian Hellman.

- Heard people sobbing in the audience while acting in Larry Kramer's *The Normal Heart.*

- Learned how to hold for long, rolling laughs in Beth Henley's *Crimes of the Heart.*

- Appeared in a whole bunch of mediocre plays that taught me the fine art of making it work, no matter what "it" was.

- Worked with both new and established playwrights on scripts that in some cases were being rewritten daily.

- Worked with great, generous, collaborative directors.

- Performed alongside some tremendous actors, some of whom later became stars, winning Tonys and Emmys.

- Learned to keep it together when someone forgot their lines or missed their entrance, or when a prop malfunctioned or someone in the audience had a sudden medical emergency.

- Played love scenes, ensemble scenes, confrontation scenes, and a death scene that required me to drown on stage without the benefit of any water. (I also once had to play a "bedroom" scene during which, thanks to a jammed door latch, the bed never actually made it onto the stage.)

- Performed a matinee with a terrible case of the stomach flu. Since most regional theatres do not employ understudies, after each scene I would calmly walk offstage and throw up into a garbage can, then return to the stage in time to perform the next scene.

- Learned to play characters from all over the planet, characters who lived in different centuries, and characters from different cultures.

- Mastered speaking in accents while cavorting around the stage dressed in frock coats, knee britches, top hat, overalls, togas, sandals, or high heels. I wore a dress in one show (more on this later). An ugly brown wig in another. A bald cap in another. I once had to pull off an entire performance caked head to toe in mud.

- Played teenagers, senior citizens, heroes, villains, the comic relief, the leading man, and the gay best friend.

- Embraced a little trouble while avoiding big trouble.

- Learned how to communicate, collaborate, concede, and congratulate.

- Appreciated the value of always being nice to everybody who works backstage or in the costume shop.

- Learned how to play cards and hold my liquor.

- And I can proudly say I've seen the sun rise over several major American cities.

And somewhere along the way, I learned a tremendously important lesson:

I was once cast in a play that wasn't particularly good. On top of being poorly written, it was physically demanding, and we weren't being paid very much for performing it. I began to feel a little resentful and didn't much care for the Saturday schedule, which forced us to perform a 5:00 p.m. show, wolf down a dinner provided by the theatre, then turn around and knock out another show with almost no break. One night, as I was climbing the stairs to the rehearsal hall where our dinner awaited us, I started complaining to a castmate.

"Could somebody please tell me exactly why we have to do this eight times a week?" I grumbled.

Suddenly, the oldest member of our cast (who was just ahead of us on the stairs) stopped, turned, and stared imperiously down at me. Looking terribly offended, he solemnly said, "We do eight shows a week, young man, on the off chance that we might get *one* of them right."

I have never forgotten his words. In subsequent years, that sentence has been my mantra about acting in general and particularly acting on stage. Every time the curtain goes up, you don't really know what awaits you. Anything could happen. All you know is that tonight, you have another chance to get it right.

The only drawback to all this wonderful work was that it went largely unseen by the New York theatre community. Notable directors, producers, and agents didn't tend to jump on a plane or train to come see you in these shows. Hence regional work tended to breed yet more regional work.

Some of my peers opted to instead stay "in town" in their twenties and act in artsy, nonpaying, off-off-Broadway shows. And in some cases that was a very wise choice, since they were seen more often and met more people, and their careers advanced a lot faster than mine did.

When I finally stepped away from theatre, I did it with great sadness. It would be many years before I would return. Even as I write this, I'm secretly hatching a plan to put myself back on stage in the next few months. Performing live on stage remains the most challenging and rewarding thing you'll ever do as an actor. Even if your focus lies entirely in TV and film, I can assure you, theatre is one of the greatest acting teachers you'll ever have. Don't miss the opportunity to learn from it. It will stretch you. It will scare you. It will exhaust you. It will reward you. It will astound you. It will make you very proud of yourself. It will teach you a lot about your craft and yourself.

Eventually, as it does for most stage actors, there came a time when I began seriously considering the possibility of acting in TV and films. Up until I was about thirty, I had basically no experience in front of a camera. I had done some extra work and an "under five" on a soap opera—meaning I had fewer than five lines (two, to be exact). I still remember them: "I have a flower delivery for Mrs. Alden" and "Thank you, ma'am." Basically, the other actor opened the door, took the flowers from me, placed a tip in my hand, and shut the door in my face. We did it in one take, and I went home. It didn't feel much like acting.

When I got my first audition for a "real" TV job on a network show in L.A., I was thrilled! The audition was for *Head of the Class*, a long-running half-hour comedy series that I'd heard of but never actually seen. This was my first extended stay in L.A., and I was determined to make an impression on somebody. I had no agent at the time, but a friend had put in a good word for me that had resulted in this audition. It was a fairly simple scene. I was playing an evil casting director, and the role required me to be super rude to the leading character of the show, who was auditioning for a movie role. Having done a lot of comedic roles on stage, I was determined to use my entire bag of tricks to dazzle these TV folks into hiring me. I worked very hard on my audition and came up with a few great bits and a couple of really hilarious eye-rolls that I was sure would bring down the house.

But when I showed up for my audition at the Warner Brothers lot, I started to get scared. The whole vibe was so different from New York. Somehow the other actors in the waiting room all looked funnier than me. I know that's ridiculous, but that's what my brain was telling me at the time. Suddenly, my name was called, and I was ushered into the producer's office to audition.

Having cut my teeth in the world of New York theatre, all of my previous auditions had taken place in large rehearsal halls, big dance studio–like spaces where you take your place in front of a folding table staffed by the director, producer, and casting director, and you try to ignore the mirrors. This was totally different. It was a very nice office with potted plants, carpeting, and a sofa. I had never acted in someone's office before. Plus, they were running a little behind schedule, so I could feel the impatience in the room. Totally thrown, I suddenly forgot every rehearsed bit of business I had prepared. I looked over at the poor guy who was the reader for the auditions, and I sort of emotionally latched onto him for all I was worth. Without my gags, I felt lost. As my comedic ship went down, this reader became my life raft, and I swam toward him with all my might. I was also painfully aware that no one was laughing. Not one laugh. I felt awful. I was totally tanking, and my poor friend who'd recommended me was most certainly going to get a phone call after this fiasco.

Finally, I finished. Slowly, I turned to face the director and casting director, who were all smiles.

"That was hilarious!" the director said.

"Thank you," I said nervously.

"Great work!" the casting director added.

Not exactly sure what had just happened, I wasted no time exiting the room. Forty-five minutes later, I got the call. I'd booked the job.

I was elated, yet terrified, since I had no idea *why* I'd been hired. What I'd done in that office had very little to do with "acting"—at least not the kind of acting I had previously done onstage in New York. I was learning the big difference between stage and camera. On camera, it's not about playing for the audience, *because there is no audience*. It's entirely about you and the actor standing opposite you.

I now like both camera and stage work for very different reasons. Stage is so luxurious. You have weeks to rehearse, followed by (hopefully) many more weeks to perform your role over and over. It's wonderful, and you get all that great applause every night.

Working for the camera operates in a very different way. Being on a film or TV set is one of the weirdest universes you'll ever encounter, mostly because nothing about the schedule or working conditions is really conducive to doing good work, yet people do excellent work in that medium all the time. I've done some of the best work of my career on TV—and hope to do more.

This is a big subject, but it boils down to this: on-camera acting is just acting—but you are not sending your performance to the back row of a theatre. The "back row" comes to you. You are just acting with and for the other actor(s) in the scene. Your performance doesn't need to travel farther than the physical distance between you and the other person (which usually is at most a few feet, often much less!). The artistry of film and TV acting is creating the purest and most truthful intimacy you can muster while a crew of forty people stand around watching. The process moves fast, so it requires you to know your lines and have a strong sense of the scene before ever arriving on set. Rehearsal time is minimal—usually designed more for the camera crew than for the actors. You have to discover, refine, and build the scene, take by take—a process that is broken up each time the camera has to be moved, and usually finishes up by shooting the all-important close-ups (during which you must be utterly focused on and working off of your fellow actor). I don't think any style of acting (particularly camera acting) can really be explained too well in a book, so I'm going to advise taking a class so you can learn how to make the adjustments needed. Trust me, it's not that hard. The best advice I ever got on the subject was from a veteran: "You can't 'act' a character in front of the camera. You have to 'be' that character."

In my opinion, if you can create truth in one medium, you will be able to create it in another.

Lastly, there are two really great reasons to pursue at least *some* camera work in your career: money and exposure. Camera work pays well, and it pays residuals (those wonderful checks I mentioned earlier that just arrive in the mail every time your episode plays anywhere in the world). Camera work is also seen by a huge audience, and if the show is well known, that camera credit can find its way into a pair of parentheses after your name—as in "David Dean Bottrell (*Modern Family*)"—and may lead to other gigs (even theatre gigs).

Five things to remember about stage and camera work:

1. Theatre can be a remarkable, fulfilling experience for any actor. If you love acting and immersing yourself in dense, amazing material, acting in theatre is something you truly need to pursue in your career. It requires stamina and a ton of skill. And yes, it can be a little tricky financially, but in the end, I believe that it is well worth any sacrifice needed to accommodate it.

2. Camera acting presents its own set of challenges, but if you understand those going in, it can be incredibly fun. Especially if you are working with TV and film veterans. There is a wonderful spontaneity and excitement to constructing and executing a scene within a limited time frame. And along with that can come a great sense of satisfaction when you walk away feeling like you left your best work "in the can," as they say.

3. If you're concerned with learning camera technique, I have some good news. Chances are you have an invaluable tool sitting in your pocket right now. Use your cell phone to videotape yourself doing a simple chore or just looking out the window for a few minutes. You'll be astounded at how powerful the simplest, smallest expression of a thought or an emotion can appear on camera. It's fascinating, empowering, and fun to learn what you can do.

4. I have never known a camera actor who didn't benefit from doing stage work. I have never known a stage actor who didn't benefit from doing camera work. Each has a different process. Each has a very different personality. Each requires focus, courage, confidence, and a real love of the craft.

5. Most actors tend to focus on one medium or the other. I think you should never get stuck in one medium too long before at least revisiting the other. It's tricky to make a living as an actor. Don't limit yourself.

**THE BEST THING ABOUT
SHOW BUSINESS?**
**As a writer, watching really pretty
actors perform the sickest, craziest,
sweetest, and angriest parts of your
brain. And getting paid for it.**

—Victoria, TV writer, series creator, and showrunner

18

HOW BAD COULD IT BE?

———

Writing That Script

Today was the day. This was it. I was going to start that damn script. I had finally landed my first big-deal writing assignment in L.A. This wasn't a rewrite or a polish. This was a new adaptation of a classy, challenging novel. I'd fought hard to get the job. I had a unique take on the material, and my employers were behind me. Yes, this was the day. Definitely. For sure. There was only one problem. I had been saying "This is the day" every morning for almost a month. I had agreed to deliver my first draft in seven weeks, and now half the allotted time was gone, and I hadn't even started. The truth was, every time I sat down at the computer, my chest would tighten. I felt nauseated and confused; my head began swimming like I was getting the flu. When I stared at the screen, visions of disaster swirled before my eyes. I'd spent the last four years of my life cajoling and elbowing my way into the screenwriting business. Now I was in it. But something was suddenly occurring to me—something that I probably should have considered before applying for the job: I had no talent.

And now for a little backstory.

Shortly after my thirtieth birthday, my acting career dried up and died. I couldn't get auditions, and on the rare occasion when I did score an appointment, I could not seem to book the job. It eventually became clear to me that I had hit one of those periods in an actor's career when you "age out of your type." Having been blessed with some pretty good genes, I'd spent my twenties playing misunderstood youths, but now I was in a weird in-between state—neither young nor old—where no one quite knew what to do with me. Soon I was back to bartending at weddings and bar mitzvahs, and not long after that I was overcome by a dark, crippling wave of despair.

With my desperation level rising daily, I realized I had to make a bold move. So I cowrote a stage play, *Dearly Departed*. My writing partner and I put together a reading and invited everybody we knew in the business. Happily, there were a couple of people who "knew people" in attendance. The play was quickly produced, first by the Long Wharf and then by the Second Stage—both very prestigious theatres—and I was suddenly launched into what would become my second career in show business: writing for a living. This led to a move to L.A. (without my original writing partner), and I found myself in a magical place where you could go into someone's office and convince them to pay you to write a script that you hadn't even started yet.

I am including this chapter about my stint as a writer for an important reason: more and more actors are creating work for themselves—plays, one-person shows, pilots, web series, independent films—and they are, in some cases, selling those projects. These new hybrid artists are literally writing their own careers.

Inexplicably, not long after my arrival in L.A. I was scooped by one of the biggest agencies in Hollywood and assigned to a heavy-hitting rep with a reputation for aggressiveness. I signed with her because (a) she really liked my work and (b) she scared the crap out of me. A self-described "no bullshitter," she'd been blessed with a fierce personality and a phone manner so forceful that I tended to hold the receiver about eighteen inches from my ear every time she called.

Initially, my new career didn't go all that well until, happily, a young producer took a chance on me. Knowing I was unproven, he initially kept me on a pretty short leash. For weeks, I was required to hand in numerous outlines and treatments (and revisions of those outlines and treatments). In frustration, I called my agent, who eventually got him off my back. At last I was free to start really writing. And that's when it happened. The enormity of the task hit me like a speeding truck, and I found myself paralyzed and drowning in self-doubt.

Finally, unable to stall any longer, I sat down and began. It was slow, excruciating, horrible work. Each sentence was worse than the one before. Each piece of dialogue as stiff and brittle as chalk. I was writing a script with no shred of inventiveness. No spark. No wit. It was total garbage. Every second spent doing it was an eternity. Finally, unable to withstand the sheer agony of it, I packed it in for the day. Even now, I'm not sure how I survived it. It was the longest fifteen minutes of my life.

The next day I returned and lasted for an hour before lunch (and maybe an hour after). In an effort to end the torture, I just started hammering it out it as fast as I could. I no longer cared what the characters said. They could say anything they wanted. I just stared at my outline and kept typing. I had no idea what I was doing. When my ex called to check on me, I confessed the sad truth.

He was skeptical. "How bad could it be?" he asked.

"It's worse than *Showgirls*," I replied. "And not as funny."

A few days later, I finally reached the end of the draft. I had before me 127 pages of *something* (I knew not what).

That night, I poured myself a stiff drink and started to read. It was horrible beyond imagining. It read like it had been written by a disturbed child. It was crap. And there was so much of it! Page after humiliating page. Then, about thirty pages in, there was a joke. I had written it spontaneously, but it was funny. A few pages past that, I found a short scene that wasn't so bad. I began to read with renewed interest. A little hope emerged. This pile of refuse in front of me was not my script. But my script was in there. I could almost see it. I just had to shovel it out. A few days before, I'd had nothing. Now, I had *something*—something I could change.

That experience taught me the single most important skill required to be a writer: the willingness to do it badly. Writing is so personal that even now I don't like admitting that there are many days when I suck at it. Every time I start something new, I always feel like I've walked into a room where the lights are off, the furniture's been rearranged, and the floor has recently been waxed. I won't do well in there initially. It's not possible. I have to give my eyes time to adjust to the dark.

It's a wonderful thing to give yourself permission to suck. It saved my career. Now, when the muse unexpectedly departs for Palm Springs midweek, leaving me talentless and alone, I've learned to just keep going. Eventually, she'll send a postcard. Years after learning this lesson the hard way, I encountered a book that explains this part of the writing process beautifully: Anne Lamott's *Bird by Bird*. (I've recommended it a zillion times.)

Throughout the history of show business, artists have taken the proverbial bull by the horns and created their own employment. It's been going on since the time of Thespis of Icaria, and it is still going on as more and more actors you've barely heard of are suddenly starring in cable shows that they've created. If you think you might have it in you to create material for yourself—a solo show, a YouTube video, a sketch show, an indie film, a TV pilot—try it! You have nothing to lose and everything to gain. Just be aware that your performer muscles will probably not really serve you well in the writing arena. It's a totally different job, and it has a ton of rules, so it's best to learn them ahead of time so you don't waste time making mistakes and learning the hard way. The best way to avoid this is to read a few books on writing for TV and film. These books can teach you the most important skill you will need to know before you can write professionally: structure.

Although most novice writers don't want to believe it, *all good writing is based on structure*. Structure is not that hard to learn. Basically, it's the skeleton. Think about your own skeleton. It shields vital organs, like your heart and lungs. All your muscles are attached to it, which allows you to stand, run, or defend yourself if necessary. If you had no skeleton, you'd be a dead, sloppy bag of skin and organs lying on the floor. I use that metaphor because I once heard a writer's script described exactly that way by a producer. You don't want that to be *your* script. Learn structure. Master it. Expand it. Bend it. But understand that it is what is keeping your script alive and moving. And be prepared to work harder than you thought you'd ever want to. It's craft. Not magic.

I worked for over a decade in the screenwriting business and was paid well for my time. Although I eventually stepped away, I have continued to write (short plays, columns, spoken word shows, and now this book). Needless to say, I love the days when the words tumble effortlessly onto the page. But that's pretty rare. In my experience, most script problems usually boil down to a writer not wanting to change something they deem "okay," because if they do, they'll be forced to replace it with some stupid, bad-sounding shit. And that's terrifying, because now you've let go of something that "sort of" worked in the hope that somehow you'll be able to spin the newly inserted shit back into gold before you have to show it to someone. No wonder writers are so crazy. What sane person would want to take that gamble? But that is precisely the chance each of has to take if we want to build a mousetrap that actually works. The great acting teacher Sanford Meisner used to say, "Bad theatre is the manure from which good theatre grows." I come from a semiagricultural background, so this speaks to me. I always assumed that writing well meant you sat down and wrote well. Now, it's the "not knowing what the hell I'm going to do" part that primarily keeps me interested in the work. It's like that song Julie Andrews sings in *The Sound of Music* about her love of brown paper packages tied up with string. Who knows what's inside there? Might be some good shit.

Eleven things I can tell you about writing a script:

1. There is never a "good" day to start. If you're waiting for that day, trust me: *it'll never come*. Just start. Once you start, stay with it.

2. It's not like any other job in the business. It requires a specific skill set and a genuine love of storytelling. Being a wonderful actor will not help you be a good writer. It requires a genuine curiosity and a willingness to start over, and over, until you find solutions.

3. Successful scripts are not about witty dialogue, clever characters, or hilarious jokes. Successful scripts are about story structure. Learn structure first. You'll save yourself a ton of time. There are many excellent books on the subject of writing for TV and film, and if that's where you're headed, definitely buy them and read them.

4. Writing requires the courage to cut sections of your script that you love but that are not serving your story and throw them in the trash.

5. Originality and fresh thought are needed at every turn. Even if it's an old plot. You're now telling it in a new way.

6. Start typing and be prepared to keep typing. Finish your script. It doesn't matter how horrible it is. Finish it.

7. Congratulations! Now you have a script.

8. Now start over. Revise. Cut the boring parts. Make the good parts great. Don't tell the audience things they already know. Work within the rules. Don't abandon the skeleton. Artfully disguise it so it becomes invisible. Beat the monster into submission.

9. Then start over again from the top. Cut. Polish. Keep going until the pages virtually turn themselves, until it reads as beautifully as your favorite novel.

10. Then let it go. Send it out into the world and see what happens.

11. If you're really fortunate, someone will want to buy your script, and they will want rewrites. If things progress, a director will join the party, and then a star, and they will also want changes. Breathe deep, and remember: these people are not your enemies. They are your new collaborators, so learn to work with them. At this point, the only goal is to try to keep the project moving forward.

One night at the Comedy Store, the comic onstage said to us, "You think this is easy? Why don't you get up here." And I did. And I was a comic for six years before I started writing comedy for TV.

—Michelle, TV comedy writer

19

STAR OF DAVID

———

The Elusive Fifteen Minutes of Fame

The young, pretty assistant director stuck her head in the door and smiled. "We're ready for you, Mr. Bottrell."

I was feeling a little jumpy, but that was to be expected. After all, I hadn't done any acting in a really long time. I exited the trailer and crossed the parking lot to where the scene was about to be shot. As I got closer, I noticed there were quite a lot of people standing around; not just crew members, but also the extras who would soon be pelting me with ad-libbed questions as my character tried to deliver his prepared statement to the press. Wow, there were so many of them. As the makeup woman blotted my face with a cold sponge, I began to feel a little short of breath. A weird numbness began crawling up the back of my neck and across my scalp. As I stared at this small army of people (all of whom were now staring back at me), I was gripped by a huge, paralyzing wave of fear. Suddenly, the director called "Action," and I couldn't remember a single word of my speech. Not one. I sputtered and stammered through take after take, never once getting it right. At one point, the poor director yelled over the cameraman's shoulder, "Just say anything!"

Finally, after about ten takes we landed one where I said most of the words in approximately the right order. I limped away, utterly humiliated. I had known the lines in the trailer! What had happened?

Before the next scene, I frantically drilled myself on every word. I arrived on the set wound tighter than a box spring. I got through it, but my performance was rigid and lifeless (and the continuity people were ready to strangle me). All I wanted was for this nightmare to be over, but there was more misery to come. My character had already been written into next week's episode. How had I gotten myself into this mess?

By answering the phone. That's how.

When my old friend Nikki Valko (one of the casting directors of *Boston Legal*) had originally asked me to audition, I had turned her down. I was scheduled to take my short film to a festival in Palm Springs, and the audition was going to screw up my departure plans. She, however, was not deterred, promising me an early appointment time and swearing it would be "fun." I agreed to come in but felt nervous about it. I had given up acting years earlier when I moved west to pursue a writing career. Occasionally, a friend of mine who was a showrunner would hire me to do a couple of lines here and there on whatever sitcom he was producing, but usually the roles were so tiny ("Customer # 2") that I didn't even have to audition for them.

When I stepped into the *Boston Legal* casting office on that fateful Friday morning, it had been more than seven years since I'd been in front of a camera. Luckily for me, I had one of those miraculous auditions that occur every other eon. Everybody laughed, and two hours later I was in wardrobe. When I received a revised script the following day, it was clear that my character (originally intended to be in only one episode) was now going to recur the following week. Apparently, David E. Kelley, the show's creator, had taken a shine to me.

A week after the debacle of the first episode, I found myself driving to the studio to shoot the second one. My knuckles were white on the steering wheel. My stomach was in a knot. I wanted to puke. Why had I said yes to this? As I flashed back on the nightmare of the previous week, I recalled one very crucial detail: everyone else on the set had been relaxed and happy. I had been the only miserable wretch in sight.

"Screw it!" I yelled out loud in my car. "I don't give a damn! I never asked for this! If I suck, it's their fault! They're the ones who hired a talentless hack for the role! I'm going to damn well relax and have fun if it goddamn kills me!"

Plastering a jittery smile on my face, I marched onto Stage 16 fully determined to stink up the joint. But fate intervened. The other actor in the scene (a series regular) was having a few justifiable problems with his character's through-line. Suddenly, the focus was off of me and onto solving his dilemma. I was all too happy to rehearse the scene several different ways until a solution was found. I began to enjoy the process, and when it finally came time to shoot my big freaky monologue (where I threatened him), I was into it. Afterward, a crew member discreetly complimented me as he unhooked my body mike. "You kinda scared me, dude," he whispered.

I was floored. Not only had I frightened the sound guy, I had actually managed to enjoy myself. The curse was broken. My one-episode character was kept on the show for eight glorious weeks, growing more nutty and sinister with each installment.

Not only was the character, "Lincoln Meyer," brilliantly written (thank you, David E. Kelley), but I was now having a field day playing him—and the viewers dug it. Soon I couldn't leave my house without being accosted by rabid fans of the show. Letters from strangers started arriving in my mailbox. I signed my first autograph, for a woman named Vera, in front of the ArcLight multiplex in Hollywood. Internet chat rooms buzzed with questions about the mysterious actor playing "Lincoln Meyer." In no time, I had an agent. Then a manager. A dear friend became my publicist. Suddenly, I was attending swanky show biz events wearing a rented tuxedo. Each week brought more TV, radio, and magazine interviews. I was even the grand marshal of a parade. It seemed everywhere I went someone was asking me about my inevitable Emmy nomination and probable win. By the time my eighth and final episode aired, I had begun to audition for TV pilots and guest star roles. Suddenly, it appeared that not only had acting welcomed me back with open arms, but it was also going to reward me with lucrative "back pay" for all the years I'd been gone.

Probably the most bizarre part of this chapter was the day that the studio sent me my fan mail. I had started receiving emails from fans relatively quickly, and at a certain point I had stopped reading them and instead started automatically storing them in a file on my computer as soon as they arrived. This, however, was an actual stack of handwritten letters. They seemed more important, since people had taken the time to sit down and pen something to me personally.

That night, I printed up all the emails, poured myself a drink, and crawled into bed with this stack of letters and messages. I took a deep breath and started reading.

Some were short notes, simply saying "We love your character" and asking for an autographed photo. Others were a little more involved. Some were quite personal. Some were genuinely poignant. Some were a little disturbing. It was a strange moment. To feel like something I'd taped on a soundstage in Marina del Rey had traveled so far and had caused all these people to take time out of their lives to track me down was new territory for me. At one point, I had to stop reading because I'd reached a point of emotional saturation. I was flooded with both awe and gratitude. All my life (or at least as long as I'd been in show business) I'd always wondered what it must be like to be famous. And now, tonight, I was getting a tiny taste of it. I also knew in that moment that this particular stretch of fame would probably be fleeting, and I was right.

In the end, although the gig brought me a generous amount of industry attention, I was not nominated for an Emmy. Most of the pilot auditions were for roles I wasn't particularly right for. Within a few months, the number of enthusiastic fans stopping me in the street began to dwindle, and little by little my life returned to normal, except that now I had one of those hyphenated careers. I was now David Dean Bottrell, writer-actor.

Truthfully, stepping back into acting hasn't been exactly like riding a bike after such a long hiatus. I'd forgotten how ridiculously brief auditions can be—not to mention the staggering number of things that can go wrong in that short period of time. Even in my early days as a stage actor in New York, I was never particularly easy to cast. I was tall and skinny, not all that handsome, and sort of quirky. I could never play romantic leads, but when cast in the right role (like a junkie or a hillbilly), I could be pretty good. The problem was finding those parts. I largely got cast because directors liked working with me and would offer me roles that I could never have booked in a standard audition situation. I was an oddball. The best theatre reviews I ever got in my life were for an absurdist play in which I portrayed a ninety-year-old man who spoke only in gibberish. When I asked my agent if he could use the good reviews to get me more auditions, he answered, "How do I sell a twenty-eight-year-old actor who plays ninety?"

When screenwriting fell into my lap, I wasn't too sorry to leave acting behind. The constant scramble to stay visible was wearing me out. The huge disappointments were getting harder to take, and then there was all that horrible waiting for the phone to ring. Although I'm a little less vulnerable now, there are still some aspects of the job that kill me. Chief among them being that godless moment when I am driving home from an audition and it suddenly occurs to me what I *should* have done—that brilliant line-reading or funny bit that would surely have landed me the job! Ugh! Sometimes I wonder how I could have invited all that anxiety and regret back into my life. I guess the answer is that when acting goes well, it's a pretty incredible feeling. For a brief shining moment, I think I understood what it must feel like to be an Olympic athlete—performing some ridiculously complex feat, but somehow doing it with an ease and precision that seems almost supernatural. And then there are the cheers from the crowd!

I have a few friends who are considered famous in that you would recognize their names if I casually dropped them in this book (which I'm not planning to do). One of them seemed sort of famous long before she actually was. She always walked into a room with a great deal of confidence, and people noticed her immediately. When she became well known, she took to the interviews, public appearances, and red carpets like a duck to water. It was an incredibly easy transition for her. If she's ever had an unhappy day in the spotlight, I've never heard about it. She's one of the happiest people I know.

Another friend of mine was not so well equipped to become famous and didn't handle it well, resulting in his somewhat awkward departure from the business. I have another friend who became überfamous and seems to have handled it pretty well. I say "seems" because I haven't actually seen this person in years, mostly because their time has become unbelievably valuable.

The second-most-famous person I know really dislikes fame. Primarily, they regret the loss of anonymity. Due to the number of their fans, going to the grocery store or dry cleaners can be challenging. For a while this person was being pursued by a truly crazy fan and had to hire twenty-four-hour security guards. According to this friend, the best part of fame has been the ability to draw attention to worthy causes and to give generously to favorite charities. Sometimes I think I wouldn't mind a little fame, just so that when my name comes up in a meeting or a phone call, nobody feels compelled to ask "David who?"

I've proudly achieved enough of a niche in the industry that twice an available TV role appeared in the casting notices using the character description, "a David Dean Bottrell type." Ironically, I wound up playing one of those roles. I once had a very talented young actor take my class because a casting director had commented that he seemed like a "young David Dean Bottrell." I was both flattered and horrified, since I was, up until that moment, unaware that I had become the "old" David Dean Bottrell. Although I'll admit there was a time in my life that I yearned for my name above the title, that time is long past. In fact, I'm somewhat grateful that I never achieved that level of stardom, since—in the eyes of the business, anyway—once you've achieved it, there is nowhere to go but down. I'll be happy if I continue to work. Period.

Having held several different jobs in show business, I can say that acting is both the best and the worst of them. On the one hand, you have a remarkable opportunity to connect with an audience in the most personal and intimate way. People love actors and feel oddly connected to them. Actors are the most well-known artists in the industry (and in some cases, the most highly paid). On the other hand, acting is an enormously precarious profession, filled with painful rejections, with very little control over one's future. Some people manage to balance all the variables and come out with a happy, balanced life. Others don't fare as well. I do believe acting is not just a career choice; it's a calling. The fame part is a little difficult to predict. If you become one of the fortunate ones who are visited by fame, here is my advice: surround yourself with the most honest, grounded people you can find. Create a family of some kind and keep them close. Use fame to further your personal and artistic goals, but make sure there's a nice, clear boundary between your public and personal lives. Make sure there's a balance.

Five thoughts about fame:

1. Most nonfamous people think it would be awesome to be famous. That's because part of the job of being famous is maintaining the illusion that famous is a great thing to be.

2. The worst thing fame can do to the few it visits is to separate them from the real world (and from any form of inconvenience). Suddenly, carrying their own belongings or standing in a line becomes history. They can find themselves surrounded by a staff of "yes" people who gradually but thoroughly brainwash their new boss that their time is as precious as gold and their comfort is more important than anyone else's. Sometimes the newly famous start to believe this fantasy as well, and before long some begin to experience a profound form of loneliness that can quickly cause big problems in both their personal and professional lives.

3. Fame is sort of like a tall building with many floors. If you are living on one of the upper floors, you can usually make a lot of money. However, there are some residents in the building who, due to their quirkiness, humor, or looks, manage to generate a lot of attention, but not necessarily a ton of money. The elevators in the Fame building are pretty busy with the residents moving up and down, depending on how their careers are going.

4. Unfortunately, fame today doesn't guarantee fame tomorrow. It's a beast that must be fed. To maintain it, you must always be thinking of where the next fertile ground might lie. Only a handful of famous artists maintain their celebrity throughout their lives. Fame has some wonderful perks, including lots of loving attention from total strangers. It can definitely give you career options (but not guarantees). Fame can also serve as a doorstop of sorts, keeping the industry at least mildly interested in you, even when you have aged out of your prime.

5. Fame, although shiny and exciting, is not what it appears to be. Fame is pressure. Fame is risk. Fame can be hard on marriages and children. But most importantly, fame is a job with long hours and few vacations, and one that requires a lot of commitment and hard work.

I ASKED A FEW OF MY FRIENDS: WHAT'S THE BEST/ WORST THING ABOUT BEING FAMOUS?

BEST THING?

House seats. Dinner reservations.

WORST THING?

Having other people tell you what they think of your work too frequently.

—Famous writer

BEST THING?

You get noticed.

WORST THING?

You get noticed.

—Famous director

BEST THING?

The best thing is people smiling when they recognize you, and saying they enjoy your work.

WORST THING?

The worst thing is hearing about your current appearance. Someone once came up and told me that his friend thought I looked uglier in person than I do on TV or film. He laughed when he said it, like he thought I'd think that was hilarious.

—Famous TV and film actor

BEST THING?

I believe true fame is when everyone's mother has heard of you. I do not possess that kind of fame. However, I have a lovely sort of quiet notoriety where just about every day some-one either on Facebook or on the street tells me that I've made an impact on their lives. I'm very grateful.

WORST THING?

It's difficult to know if someone finds you sexually attractive or just fascinating.

—Famous theatre artist

PART THREE

KEEPING THE
DOOR OPEN

Even after you've established yourself in the industry,
you're faced with the task of "staying in." Everybody is.

Sometimes this requires us to be courageous enough
to address a few things that we'd prefer to ignore.

The process of finding work is changing rapidly, and you will have to change with it. The business is more corporate now, there is less money all around—unless you are on a major network or cable channel, in a feature film, or on a Broadway stage. The competition is very intense.

—Jeremiah, leading man, musician, and series regular on iconic TV series

20

AND SPEAKING OF ME

Self-Promotion

Many people loathe this part of the business. It makes them cringe. I understand. Having been raised with the slightly misquoted scripture "Pride goeth before a fall" ringing in my ears, I have always had a weird love/hate relationship with it.

In the early days of my career, I was terrified of using the phone to solicit interviews or auditions. I couldn't bear the idea of any kind of truly personal rejection. But I was also obsessed with finding a way into the business. Thus I decided I would wage my campaign via the US mail. Around that time I had a job at a horribly mismanaged brokerage company where, unbelievably, I was put in charge of ordering the office supplies. Every month I ordered a little more than we needed, and every Friday I marched out the door with a backpack stuffed with manila envelopes, staples, markers, and stamps that I used to launch a relentless direct-mail campaign to every casting director and agent in New York. I can't tell you how many photos, flyers, letters, and postcards got dumped into the mailbox each week on the corner of Avenue A and East 12th Street. Once in a while, it actually worked! I remember booking a job at a regional theatre that had been on my mailing list for over a year. On the first day of rehearsal I ran into the artistic director in the lobby. I immediately thanked him for hiring me. Shaking my hand, he replied, "I had no choice. It was the only way I could get you to stop sending me things."

Although people do still mail photos, postcards, and flyers to agents, managers, and casting directors, promotion has (like everything else) moved into the digital age, so if you haven't already done so, be prepared to create a social media platform of some kind. A website isn't a bad idea, and you'll definitely want your own personal email list of colleagues and fans. If you're not a big social media person, ask around. Someone you know will be on top of that ever-evolving world. At present, Facebook, Twitter, and Instagram are the big ones. There's always a new platform. Ask some questions. Figure out how to use your time well. If you don't yet have many (or any) professional credits, I wouldn't suggest creating a Wikipedia page for yourself or writing an extensive personal bio for IMDB.com. Wait until there's more to say about yourself career-wise. Most newer artists don't realize there's no shame in being new. New is a good thing, provided the industry perceives you to be a new person who is active and learning more about the business every day.

I learned a great deal about social media promotion when (during my time in L.A.) I wound up in a small show that developed a massive cult following. It was called *Streep Tease: An Evening of Monologues from Meryl Streep Movies Performed by an All-Male Cast*. It was one of the most hilarious shows I've ever been involved with. It became a huge underground sensation and played at various small venues in L.A. off and on for over four years. I loved the piece I created for the show, in which I performed the entire plot of *Out of Africa* in six minutes. To keep the audiences coming, I discovered that although nobody likes to be "advertised to," most people will give you a few seconds of their time online to be entertained.

Borrowing a page from those commercials that air during the Super Bowl, I set out to keep the online promotions for the show as clever, innovative, and funny as possible. I constantly took photos and video of everything and everybody related to the show and used every scrap of Meryl trivia I could find. But after four years, I was scraping the bottom of the barrel. One night, in desperation, I took a picture of my car parked on the street and posted "Look at this great parking spot I got outside of the Bang Theater where *Streep Tease* has been playing for four years!!!" That post got five times more "likes" than the last three, which had featured photos from the show. Parking is sort of a big deal in L.A.

If you are doing something that you are very proud of, definitely promote it. Don't worry about whether professional people come or not; just make sure you get the word out, to the best of your ability. We work in a business where most of us never have the time required to see everything that we've heard is "good." I can't tell you how many times I've shown up in a casting director's office and they've said, "Sorry I couldn't make it to your show. I heard you were terrific."

And how did they hear I was terrific? Because I told them so, by sending them a steady stream of promotional material that included press quotes and audience testimonials. As I mentioned previously, talk isn't cheap.

If you land something really great (a showy part in a great venue, a recurring role on a TV show, a film that's doing well on the festival circuit), consider hiring a publicist. They are not cheap, but they can be effective. Gatekeepers tend to open their gates for (a) people whose work they have actually seen or (b) people they keep hearing about. That said, I repeat: publicists are not cheap, so hire them only for projects that can probably generate at least some publicity on their own. The publicist's job will be to magnify and build on the show's PR and single out your work for special attention.

Please make sure that whatever form your promotion takes, it is free of any kind of apology or self-deprecating remarks. I once got a flyer from someone that literally said "I know you'll never come and see this, but the show's really not half bad and I don't suck." *Do not ever send out anything that reads like that.* Whatever you're promoting, it's good, and you're good in it. Period. If you don't think so, don't promote it.

I know some people are promotion phobic. They assume that the truly talented (like [insert your favorite iconic actor's name here]) would never stoop so low. I'm sure there have been a few people who achieved success without ever having spent a minute of their time promoting their work in any traditional sense of the word. But I'll bet if they were doing something they were proud of, they found a way to drop the project into conversation while tickets were still on sale.

Again, my best advice on self-promotion is to always strive to come up with entertaining ways to promote yourself, your upcoming appearances, and your general show business persona. Just to clarify: The word "entertaining" does not always have to mean funny. It has a lot of definitions. It can mean "engaging," "smart," "sexy," "scary," "mysterious," "gritty," "human"—you name it! If you're not a big comedy person, then post material that suggests the kind of dramatic work you shine in. And remember, even if you're not currently appearing in anything, your hobbies, travels, favorite teams, family, volunteer work, and favorite authors, actors, or artists can all be fun fodder to create some interest and define your brand among your followers.

Depending on your personality, self-promotion can be as big, loud, and goofy as a drunken frat party or as small, elegant, and tasteful as a Christmas card from Buckingham Palace. Given how crowded the industry is these days, it's sort of ridiculous to ignore promotion. The best way to think of it is as a long-term investment in establishing your presence in the business. In other words, don't expect instant results. The goal is to simply keep your face and personality in circulation on a regular basis.

The ten nuts and bolts of self-promotion:

1. It's important to let the industry know what you are doing (acting in a play or a short film that's now in a festival, a stand-up comedy gig). Although you should be inviting them to come, don't expect them to. They might, but it's unlikely. More importantly, you're making it clear that you're not sitting at home wishing you had a career. You're out there doing your thing.

2. The most common way to invite industry people is via postcards or flyers sent through the US mail. You can create a flyer on your laptop and then print it someplace like FedEx Office or Staples. Postcards are pretty easy to design and order online at sites like VistaPrint.com. Whatever you are mailing, make sure your headshot (or a photo of you) is prominently displayed along with your name and contact info. If you're terrible at designing this sort of thing, ask a friend for help or hire someone. Do your best to make flyers and postcards look as sharp, professional, and appealing as possible.

3. You should write a short message on each one: "Hi Annie! I loved being in this short movie!" followed by your signature. "Hey Jack! This play is fantastic! I'm happy to get you tickets if you're free!" followed by your signature.

4. The list of people to invite should include
   a) Agents
   b) Managers
   c) Casting directors
   d) Directors (if you have some kind of personal connection)
   e) Writers (if you have some kind of personal connection)
   f) Other actors you personally know and admire
   g) Your nonindustry friends, family, and fans (you need an audience!)

5. The mailing addresses of agents, managers, and casting directors can usually be purchased in the form of mailing labels at stores like the Drama Bookstore in New York or Samuel French Bookstore in L.A. You can also order these labels online via Backstage or Breakdown Services.

6. You can also promote your current projects via social media (which is free), but keep in mind that targeted invitations—invitations sent directly to the individuals you're looking to contact—are almost always going to be more

effective. Some casting directors' offices have email addresses that are available online. Not everyone likes getting promotional material in their inbox, so keep in mind this is a crapshoot.

7. You don't have to reach out to everybody. A subscription to IMDB Pro (again, that's the professional side of the fan site IMDB.com) is not a bad investment. You can see which agents represent up-and-coming actors and which casting directors are busy with fun or important projects.

8. The all-powerful givers of employment are busy people. It's not easy to get their attention. Even if they glance at whatever promotional materials you've sent them, chances are it will receive only a few seconds of their time and attention. Whatever your message, just keep sending it on a regular basis. If your message is clear, consistent, and true, eventually it will be noticed by someone. The best message you can send is that you're busy and having a blast pursuing your dream.

9. If you are going to self-promote, have a little fun with it. And always be clear about the message that your text and photos are sending. Make yourself look good.

10. Do what you are comfortable doing, but do *something*.

**THE BEST THING ABOUT
SHOW BUSINESS?**
It feeds my soul.

**THE WORST THING ABOUT
SHOW BUSINESS?**
It hurts my soul.

—Paulina, TV and film actor; credits include
a long stint on daytime drama

21

SCHEDULED MAINTENANCE

Keeping It Together

When I was a young actor, my generation didn't really take care of ourselves. We all smoked and drank. I don't remember a single one of us having a gym membership. None of us had ever heard the term "vegan" or had any issues with gluten. Nobody went to yoga or was overly obsessed with their muscle-to-fat ratio.

Times have certainly changed. Most young actors are pretty much expected to keep themselves in shape, and for many, health has become something of a religion. Self-care is a good policy and one that all of us should certainly stay on top of as time passes.

Whoever you are—whatever age, shape, body type—please remember that your body is your instrument, and being an actor is a physical profession. It requires stamina, flexibility, and strength. So find something to do that will maintain your physical being. I don't care what, but do something daily or at least several times weekly that requires enough effort to break a sweat. Similarly, keep an eye on what kind of fuel you are putting into the machine. Whether you are working on stage, knocking out eight shows a week, or acting for the camera—where the workdays can sometimes run twelve hours or longer—you've got to be able to muster enough physical and mental energy on demand. Take care of yourself.

We also have to take care of our artistic selves. There are always stretches of unemployment. It happens to everybody, including big, highly paid artists. If the stretch is longer than you'd anticipated, you might find yourself getting a little squirrelly. Strive to avoid that. There are ways to keep yourself interested and engaged in your art form between (and during) gigs. Over the years, I've discovered some practices that have truly helped me. I'm happy to offer them to you.

Pay attention. I know that sounds simplistic, but it's important. It's true that acting and writing are both internal processes, and yes, they require us to probe around inside ourselves, but we also must become conscientious observers of what's going on around us. If we want to create truthfully, we need to stay aware of how real people actually operate in the real world. Watch strangers. Better yet, talk to strangers. Ask family members to tell you their stories. Find out a little about your coworkers or neighbors. Embrace any harmless eccentrics who come across your path. You will be shocked at how inspiring this kind of research and observation can be and how much you may draw on it in your work.

Read. Each year we spend more and more time reading bite-sized bits of information on electronic screens. For some, the concept of reading anything longer than a tweet seems like some huge inconvenience. But reading a narrative story uses the precise part of your brain that you use to act, and that part is essential if you want to write anything that anyone will want to read. Reading engages your imagination and draws you into a carefully crafted, emotionally dense world filled with keenly observed moments of truthful human behavior. What artist in their right mind wouldn't want to experience more of that? Read as much as you can. Fiction. History. Biographies. Do it! Then notice how it affects your impulse to create.

Listen. More specifically, listen like an artist. Listening is the raw material out of which all art is created. It is, quite simply, the foundation of anything good you will ever create. If you're a real actor, you must learn to lower any and all barriers between yourself and your fellow actors, so that whatever they say, how they say it, whatever is coming to you from them can change you, affect you, move you off of your center. If you really want to be a good artist, take off your headphones and listen. What do you hear? What thoughts, images, and emotions do these sounds create in you? Tune your car radio to a station you would normally never listen to. How does that music affect you? Tune in to the news station. How do the latest headlines make you feel? Happy? Sad? Anxious? Angry? Listen, notice, and allow yourself to be affected by what you are experiencing. Deepen the well. Bottom line: You can never be a great artist until you become a great listener. Curiosity is the greatest quality any artist can cultivate. It will never fail you.

Live a little. Trying to be an actor can easily consume your entire life. Don't let it. Go out and have some fun. Play ball. Take a walk. Experience nature. Go dancing. Sit by the water. Row a boat. Walk up a hill. Travel when you can. Volunteer. Have a romance. Find the dumbest hobby imaginable. Step away from the world of agents, casting directors, and producers, and act like a civilian for at least a little while every day. Live your life so when you do book a job, you'll be able to bring a little of that life into your work. It's so important.

Enjoy it. I know it probably seems ludicrous that I'd need to give this advice, but you'd be surprised how often this very simple concept gets lost in the frantic scramble to stay employed. Most of the actors I know who are steadily employed take enormous joy in the process. That joy is contagious. Directors like being around it. When it is genuine, agents and casting directors recognize it. When you have a gig, do everything in your power to cherish and appreciate the experience. These jobs are not easy to get—they are precious—so strive to treat them that way. Yes, I know acting is far from a perfect job, but it's your chosen profession, so love it as fully and as often as you are able. It makes a difference.

Four essential thoughts on the subject of maintenance:

1. Your body is not just something that carries your head around. It is an essential component to being an employable performer. Keep it as strong, flexible, and responsive as you can, for as long as you can.

2. Feed your imagination with as much good stuff as you can. Performances. Books. Music. Art. History. Poetry. Anything that fascinates you.

3. Keep learning. Cultivate curiosity. Stay passionate.

4. People seeking to get into this business are always asking how the whole "getting hired" thing works. There are many answers, but in my humble opinion, no matter what you are trying to be—actor, writer, director, composer, choreographer, you name it—there is only one thing that will ultimately get you hired as an artist: *the quality of your imagination and your ability to access it.* Learn where your imagination lives, find the door, and visit that place often.

I ASKED A FEW OF MY FRIENDS: WHAT ARE SOME OF THE WAYS THAT YOU'VE LEARNED TO TAKE CARE OF YOURSELF?

At the end of every disappointment I've experienced, I find another person hustling to get theirs, to look out for themselves. So having compassion for that behavior, that ego-driven behavior, helps me forgive and move on . . . but only after I've felt gutted, angry, and depressed.

—Susanne, TV and indie film director

Don't let show business interrupt you from living your life to the fullest. Fall in love, travel, have a hobby. Don't put your life on hold for something that might be.

—Parker, TV and film actor

Acting is a long game. Be ready for that. Patience and perseverance live very well together. Acting is only one aspect of your life, and your personal qualities and philosophies will be your most determining assets.

—Gabrielle, actor, comedian, and sketch performer

Never stop taking classes from good teachers, even when you are working in the business.

—Ivan, well-known comic actor, writer, and producer

Show business is a perpetual roller-coaster ride. When you're up, you're up, and getting roles left and right. But sooner or later that drop is coming where it'll feel like the work has dried up for a spell. Just hang on and know that as long as you keep at it, keep getting out there, keep creating content, keep learning and practicing your craft, the upswing is coming back.

—Imani, indie TV and film actor and producer

22

THE TURN SIGNAL

———

How and When to Change Lanes

When I was twenty-one, I had an awesome head of thick blonde hair and looked like I was seventeen.

When I was twenty-two, I became a professional actor *because* I had an awesome head of thick blonde hair and looked like I was seventeen.

For the next eight years, my hair and I appeared in a lot of plays, some of them sort of prestigious, and auditioned (and were called back) for several iconic movies.

When I was twenty-nine, I still had my awesome blonde hair, but I didn't look seventeen anymore and couldn't get arrested.

When I was thirty, in desperation I cowrote a play that was quickly produced off-Broadway. It was viciously panned by a critic from the *New York Times* (who I'm pleased to say is now dead).

When I was thirty-one and a half, that same play was published. It has since been produced hundreds of times and pays me royalties to this day.

When I was thirty-three, I moved to L.A. to work as a screenwriter.

When I was thirty-nine, I finally landed my first major screenwriting job that paid serious money. The movie was never made.

When I was forty, a spec script that I'd written five years earlier sold and quickly went into production at a major movie studio.

When I was forty-one, the movie came out. It wasn't exactly the movie I was hoping it would be, but it made money, and I was suddenly in demand.

When I was forty-four, I was being paid a ridiculous amount of money (per week) to work on a film script that was a complete and total mess. I worked on it for quite some time and made a nice chunk of change. It was never produced.

When I was forty-five and utterly burned out, I decided I needed to get out of show business, so I married an attorney and moved to Washington, D.C. My plan was to enroll in a seminary and become a chaplain.

When I was forty-six, I got a divorce and moved back to L.A. I was devastated and completely broke, and I had no real choice but to rejoin the entertainment industry.

When I was forty-six and a half, I wrote and directed a fifteen-minute movie (on a $9,000 budget) for which I won seventeen awards on the festival circuit. It totally altered the course of my career, and I began pursuing directing work.

When I was forty-seven, my phone rang, and two days later I was again an actor on a TV show (for which I received a lot of attention).

When I was forty-seven and a half, I was almost nominated for an Emmy.

When I was forty-eight, I began to write and perform in spoken word shows in L.A. This led to my writing columns for magazines and websites.

When I was forty-nine, I was asked to teach an acting class. I discovered that I loved teaching.

When I was fifty-two, a hairdresser on a TV show asked me what color my hair "used to be."

When I was fifty-four, I got a little bored with playing murderers on TV shows and launched a science fiction theatre festival. It enjoyed a hugely successful three-year run.

When I was fifty-seven, I left L.A. and moved back to New York, where I have continued to act on TV shows and teach. And after years of thinking about it, I started writing this book.

In my experience, there are three kinds of change:

1. *Sudden, unwanted change.* Our best-laid career plans are no match for the mighty and unstoppable forces of life. Sometimes the universe throws a curve ball. Something can happen to our health or the health of a loved one. A breakup or divorce can shake us to our core. The death of an important person in our lives, or urgent issues with our children or aging parents can take priority. Sometimes it's the loss of an agent or a producing entity that we depended on for work. Usually, we have no choice but to address or accept these events, and sometimes they can take years to resolve. One of the most gifted actors I know needed to take a break to care for a child who arrived with some very specific needs. This actor felt sure at the time that her career was over, but it wasn't. Although she is unable to work as much as she used to, she still works. She is raising a wonderful kid, and when called on to act, she always delivers.

2. *Slow change that is a result of deterioration.* This is probably the saddest form of change because, although we're aware of a problem, we don't address it. We bury our heads in the sand and hope that the issue will magically go away with little or no effort on our part. Years ago, I watched a close friend of mine slowly destroy his up-and-coming acting career due to alcoholism. When I asked him if maybe he should consider checking out an AA meeting, he laughed it off. When he began to tank his auditions, things started going downhill fast. Fortunately for him, he finally got it together and sought help. Eventually, he built a new career for himself, but it took time. I've seen similar issues with artists who couldn't quite part with recreational drugs, cigarettes, sugar, or terrible abusive relationships, until this eventually made it next to impossible for them to create anything. Once you've done physical or psychological damage to yourself, you've made what is already a tough career even tougher. Let me be clear: I've had problems in a few of these departments myself, so I'm not attempting to be preachy. I'm just saying if you need help, get it. I did.

3. *Conscious, proactive change.* This is my favorite brand of change and the one I most want to advocate. To be a good artist, you've got to keep up with whatever is happening around you. You don't have to participate in all of it. You don't have to approve of all of it. But you've got to cultivate an honest, visceral response to it. You've don't have to be an expert on every subject, but if the population is talking about something, then it merits your attention. Artists need ideas they can express. That requires you to plant some seeds and get your hands dirty in the process. Similarly, every few years we evolve into a new person. We have new life experiences.

New insights. We hear, see, and experience life in a new way. We need to express this new awareness in our work. Fear and self-doubt are the worst possible weeds in this garden, because they spread fast. The only way to keep them from ruining our work is to be vigilant in identifying them and yanking them out by the roots ASAP. Stay present. Be aware. Experiment. Make adjustments. Stay current with your world and with yourself.

Did I say there are three kinds of change? I was wrong. I just thought of a fourth.

4. *Some changes come about because we make mistakes.* Everybody makes mistakes. Most are minor and don't hold us back for long. Others can derail us for a bit and waste valuable time. One of the best actors I know blew a very big audition because he became angry at the casting director and called the guy a rather crude name (to his face). I knew this casting director. He was a dreadful person, and I honestly didn't disagree with my friend's choice of words, but I would never have had the guts to say anything like that, because the casting director was, at the time, a power-ful player in the business. When the story got around, it made my friend a hero in the eyes of his fellow actors for a while, but it did briefly set things back for him. The good news is my friend's career survived, then flour-ished. In a way, I think the incident with the casting director actually helped him on a personal level, since he realized the only way he could survive the indignities of the business was to embrace his cranky self and become known for the fierce integrity of his work. Long story short, he remains steadily employed and highly respected.

The worst mistakes happen when we allow the business to dictate our journey. Sadly, it's easy to let the inevitable disappointments the industry doles out screw with our confidence and limit our creativity and, by default, our productivity as artists. Similarly, artists often accept no for an answer a little too quickly, when maybe they should simply ask a new question, like "Where else can I sell this?"

Those of us who are in it for the long haul need to stay aware of the ebb and flow, not only of the business but also of what is shifting and changing within us. Change is inevitable. Of all people in all walks of life, we artists above all should embrace changes and see them not as threats but as opportunities to redefine ourselves and create something that could not have existed had we not stepped a little outside of our comfort zone to discover something new.

Seven short thoughts about change:

1. Change is the only given in life.
2. It is ever-present.
3. You are changing even as you read this sentence.
4. Do not avoid it.
5. Recognize it.
6. Throw your arms around it. Welcome it.
7. Put it to use.

I ASKED A FEW FRIENDS: WHAT WAS THE BIGGEST CHANGE YOU MADE IN YOUR CAREER?

Changing my name.

—Luciana, TV and film character actor

I went from improv, to sketch, to stand-up comedy. Stand-up being where I finally found my voice (even though I thought I had found it in improv/sketch).

—Leo, up-and-coming young actor and stand-up comedian

Early in my career, I was playing the "Joey" (from *Friends*) character a lot. I felt I could do more than just play the good-looking dumb best friend. I quit going out for those roles.

—Charlie, leading man on cult hit TV show

Leaving my marriage and moving from Texas to L.A.

—Gavin, leading man and series regular on iconic TV show

After an accident, working a "real job" as my dad used to say, the biggest change I've had to make in my career was to accept that less than 2 percent of all roles in film and TV are given to actors with a disability.

—Randall, character actor

I lost a bunch of weight. Which was like introducing yourself to everyone at a party and then coming back an hour later with a different name tag.

—Rafael, young leading man and series regular

Switching from actor to writer. The realization that the acting thing wasn't going to work.

—Andrew, TV writer, series creator, and showrunner

Accepting what I can and cannot do!

—Talia, TV and film character actor

I chose to continue to work independently rather than for any company or partner for too long. It has many harrowing consequences, but the freedom is unbeatable, and the talented, extraordinary people I've met and worked with along the way are varied and numerous. Sometimes I question if I made a mistake, but then I always come back to the belief that I was on the only path I could ever have been on. The right one.

—Jessica, TV and indie film producer

**THE BEST THING ABOUT
SHOW BUSINESS?**
Going to work always feels
like going to a party.

**THE WORST THING ABOUT
SHOW BUSINESS?**
Sometimes the party
starts at 4:00 a.m.

—Helen, veteran TV comedy actor

23

LUCKY YOU

———

The Science of Getting a Break

A few years ago, it became clear that the agency I was signed to was struggling. There seemed to be a parade of new employees in and out the door each month, which is never a good sign. As a result, my auditions had dwindled to almost zero. I was getting a little concerned, since (as is true for many performers) my health insurance is dependent on earning a certain amount of money as a union actor each year.

Around this time, I got an email invitation from a friend to attend a screening of his film at a small festival being held at a theatre near me. Truthfully, I didn't want to go. His movie was very good, but I'd already seen it twice, and I didn't really want to sit through it again. I considered not going, but then my conscience got the better of me. I decided I would go to the prescreening reception, where I would find my friend and give him a big hug; then I'd slip out the side door before the screening started. That way my friend would distinctly remember seeing me there, and I could go home and work on my own movie script, which sorely needed my attention.

On arrival, I found the underground parking garage was jammed and I was forced to park on the lowest level. Having been to this theatre many times, I knew how rotten the elevator system was, so I immediately felt my resentment level rising. "No good deed goes unpunished," I heard myself say as I pushed the elevator button over and over, hoping that would speed things up. Finally, the elevator arrived and I stepped inside. Just as the door was about to close, I saw a guy darting between the parked cars, hoping he might make it to the elevator before it departed. I decided to show a little mercy and at the last second hit the "Open Door" button. Once inside, he breathlessly thanked me, and we made elevator small talk until we reached the top floor where the festival was being held. Just as we stepped out of the elevator, he commented, "I'm always so surprised that you don't speak like that character you played on *Boston Legal*." It turned out he was an agent who worked for a very established company. More chat followed, questions were asked, answers were given, and by the time we picked up our tickets for the reception, he'd handed me his card.

Long story short, he became my new agent, and over the next couple of years he managed to score me a few very important jobs that helped redefine my image within the TV casting community. All because of a chance meeting in an elevator.

Whenever I tell that story, my fellow actors tend to say, "Wow, that was so lucky!" Not to sound ungrateful, but I'm not a huge believer in what's often called "luck." After a lot of thought on the subject, I now tend to think that when unexpected things happen, and they turn out well, we call them luck. I'll talk more about the happy elevator story in a minute, but first let's talk about luck.

You may have already heard this, but artists are impatient, impulsive people, and sometimes they want to believe there's a way to speed things up. And certain folks (I'm not naming names) do all kinds of crazy things, hoping to improve their "luck."

Frequently, when people want to lure luck to their corner, they'll obsess on stories about random events that happened to other currently successful people and assume there's a secret formula embedded in those tales; a code that, if deciphered, can be reused to bring similar good fortune to themselves.

That code doesn't exist. Sometimes what appears to be magical intervention isn't really magic at all.

Let's return to the happy elevator story for a minute.

Yes, it was definitely fortunate that my soon-to-be new agent and I crossed paths in that parking garage, but there was a little more to it than that.

In truth, I wound up getting a new agent because

1. I'd done some work in the past that I was proud of.

2. I was in that parking garage because I'd come to support some good work done by another artist.

3. I held the elevator door for another human being because that's always a nice thing to do.

4. I struck up a conversation with a stranger standing next to me.

5. I noticed his interest.

6. I didn't beg for his card, but just let him know that I was open to talking to a new agent.

7. I called him the next day and set up an appointment.

8. When I arrived at the meeting, I was friendly. I was happy to talk a little about non–show business subjects, but most importantly, I was ready to offer my potential new agent a clear vision of the kind of work I now wanted to do as an artist.

I could easily tell you a bunch more stories about "lucky" unexpected turns in my career, but in reality most of them came about as a result of being involved in my community and always striving to improve my product. If that is sincerely what's going on with you, good things will probably start happening, and some of them will happily arrive without warning.

As I mentioned at the beginning of this book, this is a gambler's business, with absolutely no guarantees of success. However, if you are talented, skilled, and enthusiastic about your life, chances are luck will visit you. Then it will desert you. Then it will return, unannounced and out of the blue. Such is the business of show. Just keep going. As the late great Oscar-winning actor Walter Matthau once said, "All you need in this business is seven or eight really big breaks."

For many years I have courted, begged, chanted, and prayed over the subject of luck, and I've learned a lot. So . . .

Here are the ten things I know about attracting luck:

1. In a nutshell: Do your best work. Then do all in your power to get that work seen. This could lead to opportunities to show your skills to a new potential employer.

2. Don't get cocky: An opportunity is not a job offer. You can easily blow it if you walk in the door assuming this is destiny knocking on your door, or if you are not prepared to demonstrate your sincere willingness to work hard and collaborate.

3. Disclaimer: Occasionally, lazy, clueless people win at this game because they were absolutely, without question, born to land a particular job. It happens. It's rare. It's unjust. But it happens. Just ignore that person and move on with your plans.

4. Get better: Just get better and better. Luck really likes that.

5. Initiate: Don't wait for the phone to ring. Luck favors self-starters.

6. Network: Luck rarely walks up and rings the doorbell. You have to go out there to run into it.

7. Be ready: Most of us usually experience luck because we've trained like an Olympic athlete for these moments of opportunity and can demonstrate our artistic prowess on demand with some amount of confidence.

8. Show up: Support other artists.

9. Remember: Most stories of "luck" are about the moments when (as the Roman philosopher Lucius Annaeus Seneca observed) "preparation meets opportunity."

10. Prepare: Stay ready. Those moments are coming. Be patient.

I ASKED A FEW FRIENDS: WHAT WAS THE GREATEST PIECE OF LUCK YOU EVER HAD IN YOUR CAREER?

Crashing a lunch and meeting my writing partner (and best friend) of twenty years.

—Victoria, TV writer, series creator, and showrunner

Booking a really big recurring guest star role on a major TV show [when I had] almost no credits.

—Rachel, stage and TV actor

I auditioned for a national tour, which I didn't get, but the director was also directing a show coming to Broadway, which I did wind up getting. He's been in my corner ever since.

—Claire, musical theatre and TV actor

Getting involved with a group of misfit young people like myself who were all told they were unemployable. We shared a common dream, loved and respected each other, and a miracle happened. A show we put on for $35 moved to a commercial run and became an enormous hit. I've worked ever since.

—Laurence, iconic New York theatre performer and playwright

The greatest stroke of luck I've received was to be a mixed-race kid in the twenty-first century. I have many opportunities now because of the hard wins my predecessors fought their whole lives for.

—Taz, up-and-coming young actor and recent drama school grad

I was ushering for an off-Broadway show when a very big director approached and asked me if I was an actor. When I told him I was, he invited me to his apartment on Central Park South the next day to read opposite a big music star he was thinking of casting in a new show he was directing on Broadway, and this would be her audition. I went the next day and read with her. Shortly afterward, he offered me a job as an understudy in the production. That was how I made my Broadway debut.

—Roz, popular theatre, TV, and film actor

Getting a phone call at 8:00 p.m. one night to do extra work on a commercial to fill in for someone else who'd canceled. Then showing up to the set the next day and getting "upgraded" to principal and making $30,000 from it in the next two years.

—Mike, actor and writer

Walking into a casting session with a shit attitude and getting cast in the biggest role of my career because that's exactly what they wanted for the character.

—Gavin, leading man and series regular on iconic TV show

Having a client in a show that ran for twelve years.

—Marilyn, veteran talent manager

All of it. It was all luck.

—Charlie, leading man on cult hit TV show

Meeting a friend of mine who is a successful actor, writer, and improviser. He introduced me to a world of people who I've learned so much from. (You, Dave, being one of them—I love you dude!)

—Leo, up-and-coming young actor and stand-up comedian

Running into my favorite director in the street when I was in film school. I managed to turn that into my first job.

—Adrienne, veteran screenwriter

A director of a new movie saw me performing during a sketch comedy show and cast me in his film.

—Ivan, well-known comic actor, writer, and producer

I was in an elevator on my way up to an audition alongside a gentleman who was wearing a Mickey Mouse tie. I couldn't help but compliment him on it. Then, a little later, as I was leaving my audition to go home, I saw that same gentleman preparing a room. He was trying to unfold a table, and I asked if he needed help. Later, he said that I looked right for a role in his show. I told him I would love to audition and sang a song, a cappella. The next day, I got cast as the lead in his musical. But the really lucky part was that his best friend saw the show and cast me as Cinderella on tour. Looking back, the Mickey Mouse tie must have been a sign that we were meant to meet . . . or just a coincidence.

—Sarah, up-and-coming young actor and recent drama school grad

Going to an open call I saw in *Backstage* after working a double shift. Six hundred people were there, but I stayed and auditioned. Long story short, I got my first big break—a movie with a very big director. Worked with him off and on for ten years. He made my career. Indebted to him forever.

—Talia, TV and film character actor

Booking a huge national voice-over campaign two years in a row. I auditioned in my underwear from my home studio and sent three versions, two based on their specs and one of my own. They liked my version of the read.

—Santiago, TV actor and voice-over artist

Having a terrible childhood and the balls to write about it.

—Michelle, TV comedy writer

It's hard sometimes to be friendly with women who are "my type." Because I'm a minority, it feels like there can only be a few of us succeeding. Like, what if she gets to be known as the "hot Indian girl" before I do? Recently, I've realized that's total BS, and by engaging with others who are more like me, we discover just how different we are and how supportive we can be for each other.

—Maya, actor and voice-over artist

24

PEOPLE WHO NEED PEOPLE

―――

Navigating Relationships

I recently had a dream in which I was traveling in a car with three acquaintances from show business. In real life, none of these people have ever been particularly nice to me, but in the dream, they seemed suddenly very friendly. Although suspicious, I very much wanted to believe they were sincere. In the dream, we stopped at a gas station and went inside to buy snacks. I was the last to check out, and when I reached the counter I discovered that my companions had left a few half-eaten candy bars lying there. When the clerk saw them, he assumed they were mine, so I wound up having to pay for them. Then, when I stepped outside, I discovered that my "friends" had driven away without me. The dream ended with me in a murderous rage, screaming obscenities at their car as it disappeared over the horizon.

This dream is about show business. You're probably thinking it's about quite a bit more than that, but trust me, it's about show business. The dream is about the same issues that emerge and reemerge, over and over, in the lives of creative people. Issues like trust, loyalty, abandonment, loss, jealousy, blame, and betrayal. Given the ups and downs that most of us weather daily, it's a wonder we don't all have this dream every night. The dream is a reflection of one of the most baffling aspects of the entertainment industry: our relationships with each other.

The ingenious Martin Mull once called show business "high school with money," which is astoundingly accurate. The speed with which you can fall in and out of favor is enough to make anyone a neurotic mess. As I mentioned earlier, when I experienced a little "D-List" TV celebrity, I suddenly found myself invited to parties hosted by big, famous people I didn't really know. I got to stand on some very nice lawns and make chitchat with successful strangers who oddly treated me like a dear friend. I found this a little unsettling, though I shouldn't have. In the upper echelons of the business, this brand of rapid-fire intimacy is the coin of the realm. I once worked with a movie producer who was brilliant at it. Whenever we ran into somebody he felt he "knew" (which was about every twenty minutes), he would immediately douse that person with a big bucket of drippy enthusiasm. Then before they could wipe it from their eyes, he'd put them through a fast but thorough interrogation to see if there was anything they were doing that could in any way further his goals for the week. It rarely produced any useful information, but we are nothing if not hopeful in this industry.

Many of my most treasured friendships are with people I've met in the trenches. Having chums in the business will help keep you sane. These kindred spirits can inspire you and keep you from jumping off a bridge when you fail to get that job you wanted so much, or more importantly, when you *do* get that magical job and it turns out to be a big, horrifying nightmare. Who will buy you a beer, drag you out to a movie, or offer you a shoulder to weep upon? Your friends—who know exactly how you feel. Show business can be a rocky ride, but I will say this about it: it's filled with some fantastically loyal and compassionate comrades. They are the best.

And now for a couple of confessions.

Sprinkled throughout my address book are a few names that inspire intense feelings of jealousy, terror, and, in a few cases, loathing. This, of course, raises the question, Why would I hold onto the contact information of someone who, the second I encounter them, makes me feel like an angry, self-consumed teenager? I cannot explain my feelings or why those names remain in my roster of contacts, other than to say I suppose I don't want to admit that their behavior (or in some cases, just their creepy face) irks me so much. So I mostly just avoid *any* contact with them. In my experience, most of the truly horrible people are eventually sifted out—unless of course they are brilliant at what they do, in which case we all just have to put up with them until they die.

This might also be a good time to admit that I've not always acted with the utmost generosity and graciousness toward my peers. There are a couple of situations I wish I could do over. None of us wants to compromise our best self, but show business is a crowded industry. In the frantic race for employment or acknowledgment, it can often feel like you and everybody you know are all trying to get a seat on the last helicopter out of Saigon. In the flurry and frustration of the moment, your elbow can easily wind up in somebody's eye—and vice versa. Hopefully, they will forgive you, but they might not. Show business, for all its glitziness, winds up being an internal journey, and, like it or not, it will eventually show you what you're made of.

At the risk of sounding like a big know-it-all, I'd also like to offer a couple of thoughts about artists and their personal (aka romantic) relationships. I say this because the lives led by artists are somewhat different from those of people with regular schedules and realistic goals.

When I was a very young man, I had a wonderfully cute boyfriend who lived waaaaaaay out in Queens. I'm talking the next to the last stop on the E train. It took me almost an hour to get from my place in Manhattan to his. He was a great guy, a totally regular Joe who was studying at St. John's University to become a pharmacist, just as his father and brothers before him had done. He had no real knowledge of show business, and I—and this might surprise you—had no real interest in the pharmaceutical industry. Despite our differences, we stayed together for three tumultuous years. But by our third year together, something strange had begun to happen. Around this time, I was getting a lot of stage work, and almost like clockwork, I found myself arriving at the theatre on opening night, furious because I'd just had a big fight with my boyfriend. Finally, the penny dropped that these arguments always happened just when I most needed to be focused on work. When I asked him about the timing of these dustups, he had the guts to come clean, saying "I just feel like your opening nights are more important than I am."

I stared at him, blinked a couple of times, and told him the truth: "They are. I mean, unless you're in the hospital or something, opening night will always be more important than you, or my mother, or America, or anything."

My boyfriend's expression hardened, and his voice got quite a bit louder. "Are you saying you don't care how I feel?!"

"No!" I shouted back. "Do you think I'd ride the E train two hours a day for somebody I didn't love?? But once in a while, I've got to be an artist. I work really hard for these opportunities. And if I don't give them everything I've got, they're wasted! That doesn't mean I don't love you and want to be with you!"

My boyfriend didn't look very happy at that moment. "You could at least say you're sorry!"

I took a deep breath. "I could, but I'm not sorry! I mean, I'm sorry you're hurt! But this is my life. This is just how it works."

A few months later, we parted company when I discovered he'd started sleeping with one of his roommates, who was eighteen and didn't speak particularly great English. My former boyfriend didn't much like the idea of me shining my light on anything but him, and I suspect that (at least for a while) he got to be the center of that kid's world.

I offer this story because it takes a particular kind of person to love a professional artist, and to put up with our habits, ego, obsessions, mood swings, financial issues, and nutty schedule. I sometimes think artists should marry only their fellow artists, but then I remember the number of creative folks I know who have been happily wed to "civilians" for many years. Whoever you cast your lot with, just make sure that you can be honest with them. Artists have a lot to process, and they need to have a home where everything can be out on the table. There also must be an intellectual, emotional, and physical chemistry that will keep you drawn to your partner. It is easy to get distracted, so make sure you keep up your half of any bargain you strike with them. And keep in mind, finding that person might take some time.

This brings me to the best advice I have to offer you. If you must be an artist to be happy, then you will need to be with someone who gets that and understands that they are not in competition with your work. In a perfect world, they also have something in their life that makes them happy and that they are equally connected with. If you're looking for a life partner, keep your eyes open for someone who has patience and a sense of individual purpose (separate from you and your goals) and can see the humor in what will no doubt turn out to be a life filled with surprises.

It's a wonderful thing to share the journey, but it's no guarantee of bliss. Having been both married and single for long stretches of my life, I can honestly say I've truly enjoyed both. I can also tell you if you are not happy *without* a romance, you will not be happy *with* one. Living a rich life filled with love, family, and rewarding work is totally possible for a professional artist—provided you truly believe it can all coexist, and that each department can naturally feed into the others.

Four final thoughts about professional and personal relationships:

1. Take care of your comrades. The old song lyric "There's no business like show business" is true. I don't think there is any other business that makes less sense and is so deeply personal to those who have chosen to pursue it. Because of that, creative people can develop a very specific kinship, sort of an understood shorthand that we all have with each other. Although you

won't like everybody you meet, if you last long enough, you begin to see other actors not as competition but as fellow travelers on this odd road. If you learn to laugh with your comrades, you'll have a much better chance of staying in the business.

2. One of the trickiest parts of our profession is the asking of favors. I hate asking business favors from friends because it often places the other person in a very awkward position. That doesn't mean you should never ask, but be prepared for the "Sorry, I wish I could help" response. It's not that we don't want to help each other—frequently we do. But our ability to do so is almost always connected to the timing of the ask. When I'm asked by a young actor for an introduction to a casting director or agent, often it's not possible for me to do so. Usually, the individual they are asking me to approach is hugely busy, not currently taking new clients, or unlikely to meet with anyone who is still in the starting gate. Every creative professional has only so much "capital" in the business, and we have to be careful how we spend it. In a game where relationships can mean the difference between working and not working, we have to be careful not to come off as unaware of the other person's priorities. And in some cases, we simply need to hang onto what little capital we've earned to advance our own careers. So if you ask someone for a professional favor and they can't deliver it, try not to judge them too harshly. It's a slippery slope.

3. I've mentored a lot of young people in my business, and it has been a total pleasure to do so. Periodically answering questions, offering advice, and giving encouragement to someone who is finding their way in the industry is easy and good for the soul. Many established actors will be happy to meet a newcomer for a coffee and offer them their experience and a couple of suggestions. Sometimes this can evolve into real friend-ships that last decades. Nothing makes me happier than to see one of these young actors succeed (and their success usually has more to do with their talent than with my advice!). Never be afraid to ask your more experienced peers for guidance. Most will be happy to help.

4. On the personal front, keep in mind that you belong to a particular tribe. Artists see and feel the world somewhat differently from the rest of the population. Our passions can sometimes overcome our better judgment. We can be impulsive and a bit obsessive, and sometimes a little short-sighted. Those qualities are actually part of what makes us good at what we do, but our art is not the sum total of our lives. Even when the industry is keeping us very busy, we need to make space for families, partners, and children. Our fellow artists are great fun and will usually forgive us for being distracted or absent from time to time, but our inner circle will be expect-ing a bit more from us. Try not to disappoint them.

I know people with three-million-dollar overall deals who are bitter as f**k. If you are struggling to break in and you wonder how that's possible— well, they are comparing themselves to mega-superstars who just got ten times that.

—Stephen, TV and film writer and producer

25

DEATH BY RESUME

———

Jealousy and Competitiveness

As I stepped out of my aging Honda, I took a deep breath. I was arriving at a housewarming in one of those beautiful neighborhoods in West L.A., hosted by a friend who'd been experiencing some really big success lately. He is, in addition to being very talented and deserving of this success, a genuinely nice guy. Having super successful friends can sometimes be a little tricky for me. I'm always happy to see them recognized and rewarded, but it does have a way of making me a bit self-conscious about my own somewhat modest position on the game board. My resume, which was perfectly fine the day before this party, now seemed a bit lackluster as I stood in my friend's extremely nice living room, rattling my ice cubes. When my host spotted me talking to no one, he dragged me across the room and introduced me to another social misfit. I could tell right away that I wasn't going to like this guy. He was easily twenty years younger than me and had that sort of ambitious, disconnected edge that always makes me want to leave show business and join a monastery.

Our host introduced us to each other as "fellow writers" and sailed away. Lifting his drink to his lips, the guy asked me what sort of stuff I wrote. While I was telling him, I noticed his eyes drifting over my shoulder as he scanned the room for someone more interesting to talk to. Ordinarily, I wouldn't have cared, but I'd had two vodka tonics by then, and having nothing better to do, I decided to screw with him.

"Hey," I said, feigning interest, "I think I've heard of you." This being Hollywood, his eyes instantly snapped back to my face. I now had his full attention. For the next ten minutes, as soon as he would mention one of his credits, I would mention one of mine. Each volley had the sole purpose of one-upping the other guy. Soon we were discussing projects that didn't even exist yet. It was a total standoff, until suddenly a famous actor broke into our conversation to say how much she'd enjoyed my performance on a TV show I'd recently appeared on. We struck up a conversation, and after about sixty seconds of being utterly ignored, my opponent fled the scene. Victory was mine. In the game we were playing, being recognized by someone famous is sort of like a royal flush. It beats anything the other guy's holding.

This little episode raises the question, Why would two grown men get involved in such a ridiculous pissing contest while attending a friendly little Hollywood party? Why would each feel the need to keep spewing his credits (even unproduced credits!) just to advance a game that can never be won? The sad reasons for this include seriously bruised egos and crappy self-esteem, but there is a bigger truth at work. We were both standing in the very expensive living room of a mutual friend who was currently doing extremely, extremely well.

To stay in this business, you have to, by nature, be a fighter, and fighters need to win sometimes—even if the battle is ridiculously petty. I have no doubt that had Mother Teresa gone into show business she would have sold the whole convent down the river for a development deal and never thought twice about it. Like it or not, our less attractive personality traits, like competitiveness and aggression, are actually necessary sometimes just to get a leg up. The trick is knowing when and how to stop using them once the goal is achieved. We all want to be one of the cool kids. It's tough to let go.

Jealousy, however, has no useful purpose that I'm aware of. Coveting somebody else's career stops you dead in your tracks. It wastes precious time, blocks creative thought, and generally makes us hate our own guts. Having been in show business since the 1850s, I've worked with and befriended many talented people over the years. Some of them have gone on to really big successes, winning Emmys, Tonys, and Oscars along the way. Was I always thrilled to hear their good news? No, not always. I'm talented. I'm funny. I'm cute (well, sort of). Why them and not me?

When I was a young actor in New York, I once auditioned for an off-Broadway show that I really wanted. The role went to someone else, a young actor named Kevin Bacon. *Who the hell is Kevin Bacon?* I thought. Then Kevin Bacon started making movies, and I wasn't too happy about that development either. Kevin Bacon (whom I've never met, by the way) is exactly my age. We are approximately the same height and have the same hair color, but that's pretty much where the similarity ends. He is, I'm told, a very nice guy who has done some truly fantastic work in film (like *The Woodsman*, for example), giving performances that I could never have come up with in a million years—because I am not Kevin Bacon. I'm me. I'm not saying I'm a talentless schmuck or undeserving of recognition. Quite the opposite. I'm proud of what I do, and always feel very happy when I'm doing it. Funny thing, but whenever I am busy, I'm generally not too concerned about how everybody else is doing.

Sadly, this is not true for everyone.

I was once shooting a guest star role on a TV show. Also in the scene was an actor who had costar status (meaning she had a smaller role that paid less money). The scene was a little complex and had a few moving parts to it. It required some concentration, and it could have been a fun way to spend the morning, had this woman not been so obsessed with grilling me and every other actor on the set with a thousand questions.

"Who is your agent? Are they taking any new clients?"

"Have you ever auditioned for this casting director?"

"Do you have a manager? Can I contact her? Can I use your name? What's your email address?"

I kept trying to dodge her, but she was obsessed with trying to extract every detail of how I'd achieved guest star status. I truly don't mind trying to be helpful to my fellow actors, but this woman was coming off like some kind of investigator from the fair employment commission. Finally, I politely but firmly asked her to hold all further questions until we were through shooting. Embarrassed and angry, she then made a point of making snide little comments to the background actors in the scene, just loud enough for me to hear them. They mostly centered on the condescending attitude of "Mr. Guest Star."

At the end of the shoot, I marched up and calmly said, "You said you wanted business advice. Do you still want it?"

Not surprisingly, she declined my offer and fled the scene. Had she stayed, this is what I would have said to her: "You had a job today that a zillion actors would have loved to have booked. And instead of enjoying it, you were so obsessed with how to land my job, you ruined the experience for yourself and everybody around you. And you then acted like I'd disrespected you, when the real problem was you let petty jealousy rob you of what could have been a really fun day."

Look, we're all human. It's natural to thirst for a little recognition or a bit more money. But there is a big difference between envy (which won't kill you) and jealousy (which sort of can). To quote the wise words of the twenty-fifth and twenty-sixth president of the United States, Teddy Roosevelt, "Comparison is the thief of joy." So do yourself a favor and avoid measuring yourself against others—especially your friends. In truth, there is no comparison. The factors that generate creative success are so varied and complex that not even the late great Stephen Hawking could have broken them down into an understandable equation. Your career is uniquely your own. Let me repeat that: *Your career is uniquely your own.* It will never bear any real resemblance to anyone else's path. Claim it and get back to work. Unearth something new. Go forward. There is no shortage of adventures to be had in this business. So get busy.

I have three things to say about jealousy:

1. It's a total waste of time and energy.
2. Learn to release it quickly by focusing on something else. Your own work, for instance. Or maybe something other than show business that genuinely interests you.
3. That artist didn't steal anything from you. You have new work to do. Go discover it.

I ASKED A FEW FRIENDS: HAVE YOU EVER BEEN HELD BACK BY JEALOUSY?

I have learned that I can never get back the time I wasted being jealous/angry/upset that someone else got something. Time is so valuable, and it's better spent on self-improvement and moving forward. Jealousy sidelines you.

—Gabrielle, actor, comedian, and sketch performer

I used to sit around and scream at the TV, "Why that guy?!?!" Then one day you meet "that guy," and he's great. Then you think, "I'm an asshole." Lesson learned.

—Charlie, leading man on cult hit TV show

No; jealousy is one of the best fuels for an actor and will only help you succeed.

—Mike, actor and writer

Ego and jealousy held me back from trusting others to help me. It cost me sleep and sanity. Now I've learned to let your ego go and let others help you succeed.

—Victoria, TV writer, series creator, and showrunner

Comparing myself to other actors held me back even when I was successful. I felt unmotivated, because I kept thinking that I wasn't good enough to have what they had. I've learned to remember why I want to act in the first place—to give back. Now, instead of comparing, I've learned to observe and support my peers.

—Sarah, up-and-coming young actor and recent drama school grad

Compare and despair is a bad habit, and it will get you nowhere. There will always be someone more talented than you, but being the most talented is not what it's about. For me, I work in a very spiritual and heartfelt way. I know that I can bring a beautiful and rich depth to my characters. So I focus on that. It brings me joy, and joy gets me work.

—Claire, musical theatre and TV actor

Jealousy is teaching me lessons every single day.

—Taz, up-and-coming young actor and recent drama school grad

I'm jealous of everyone, and it hasn't hurt me one bit. You can't let it warp your perspective or stop you. Try and allow your jealousy to inspire you to dig deeper.

—Laurence, iconic New York theatre performer and playwright

It is hard not to be envious. Concentrate on your work instead of what others are doing—if it means taking a break from social media, then do it. But keep the focus on yourself.

—Nina, Broadway theatre actor and comedian

Envy is a tough one. For years I couldn't read the trade papers because it ate me up. Then I found out Mike Nichols at the peak of his career had the same problem, so I decided I was fine just not reading the trades.

—Adrienne, veteran screenwriter

There have been auditions for shows and films that I've come very close to getting and been so disappointed when someone else was cast that I refused to watch the completed project once it's released. I've learned to get over that and to watch the show and to see what choices they made that were different from mine. Not necessarily better choices, just different, and it's interesting to see how that changed the character. It's actually a great learning tool.

—Imani, indie TV and film actor and producer

Any time I've ever passed a billboard for a job I auditioned for but didn't get. It's a sinkhole. You can't hold onto the past, and that includes past auditions. You just have to remember that that wasn't your job.

—Rafael, young leading man and series regular

**Learn how to manage your
own anxiety. If you can't, maybe
become an accountant.**

—Vanessa, TV writer, show creator, and showrunner

26

ROADSIDE ASSISTANCE

———

Asking for and Accepting Help

On my fiftieth birthday, the guy I was casually dating broke up with me. Truthfully, the relationship was so casual, there was no real reason he should've even known it was my birthday. I suspect that he was probably dating someone else simultaneously and simply needed to make a decision. But when he made his exit, it was like an unexpected, extremely painful punch in the gut.

A depression descended on me that I tried hard to ignore. On I went, smiling and showing up for work and social occasions, but inside I was hiding a feeling of deep sorrow. It wasn't just not having a significant other. It was a terrible feeling of having somehow missed a bigger boat. The work I was getting wasn't exactly what I'd hoped for, and it seemed as if the L.A. party was over. Although Hollywood still seemed "friendly" to me, apparently it no longer wanted to date me either. I felt like damaged goods.

The only person I felt comfortable discussing this issue with was my best friend, Tom, who is not an actor or a writer, but a real estate broker who grew up in L.A. (in close proximity to the business). "Therapy," he kept saying. I chafed at the idea. I had spent a lot of my thirties in therapists' offices and felt like there was nothing left to talk about. Finally, when I started screwing up appointments, I decided to return.

Initially, I tried to get back with my former shrink, Carrie. She was my first California therapist (and also a former model and ex-heroin addict), and I had truly loved working with her. Carrie was a stunningly gorgeous blonde; she looked like someone had put Kim Basinger on a rack and stretched her to about six feet tall. My favorite part of seeing Carrie was the magical moment when she opened the door to her office and welcomed me in. She had a jaw-droppingly beautiful wardrobe, and I never saw her wear the same outfit twice. Her taste was exquisite, so no matter what sort of ugly thing I needed to talk about, I at least had something beautiful to look at. But sadly, she was no longer on my insurance plan.

This led me to the office of Darryl, a stocky, fatherly-looking guy who was about my age and quite a bit less glamorous than Carrie. Darryl was patient and asked tough questions. Over his career, he had worked with quite a few show business types, and he had a keen understanding of the ups and downs of a creative career. One day, as I was spewing some self-defeating, bitter crap, he stopped me and said, "You know, you keep coming in here and telling me about these jobs you've booked, and you make it sound as if some sort of mistake was made. It's as if there were no other actors available in the entire city of Los Angeles, so they were somehow forced to hire you. Do you know how many actors could've played that role? Quite a few. But they chose you. You need to think about that."

And I did.

Darryl had pointed out the baby elephant in the room. I had slammed into the difference between what I had expected in my personal and professional life and what had actually happened. Over the next few months, I slowly started to sort out and define the real problem: I felt talented. I felt smart. I felt worthy of bigger, higher-profile work. I felt I deserved to be playing in the big league, but I had very little evidence to support my position. Yes, I had a roof over my head. Yes, I was paying my bills, but from an emotional standpoint, it felt like my abilities (that I had worked so hard to refine) weren't improving the credits on my resume or the size of my bank balance. On my worst days, I felt like I had been robbed—and that I was the one who had committed the robbery.

For a time, acknowledging this long-buried terror seemed to make it worse. In fact, it felt awful. It was as if whatever lifeboat I'd managed to stay afloat in had now sprung a thousand leaks. Finally, Darryl, sensing my rising panic, said, "You know, David, there comes a point in life, where there's really only one question worth asking, and that's 'What's next?' "

It took me a little while to wrap my head around the rather profound point he was making. I had made the mistake of thinking that things "hadn't worked out." In fact, they had worked out. Just not like I had expected. All of my efforts as an artist had led me to a considerable amount of skill, but skill is no guarantee of a steady stream of paychecks. My resume was highly respectable, if not stellar. I had options. Lots of them, in fact.

Out of this came an eye-opening realization. At the end of the day, I still had my talent. It was mine. I had earned it. Darryl's question became so profound, it was as if I could see it stenciled on my bedroom ceiling every morning when I woke up. "What's next?"

I began writing again. Not for Hollywood, but for myself. Soon I had a column. Then I had two. Then I had three. I began teaching. I created a one-man show: a seventy-five-minute exploration of what the word "love" means to us at various moments in our lives. It ran for eighteen months in L.A. to full houses. I was offered a job directing a play at a professional Equity theatre. Because this was L.A., I was absolutely certain that it would not advance my career. I took it anyway. It was an amazingly fulfilling experience. I created a science fiction one-act play festival that ran for three years to rave reviews. When I got an audition for a TV role, I stopped trying to get the part. I just tried to be a good actor for the four minutes I was in the room. As a result, I got better parts. And I began to take a good long look at where I was in my life and how it felt to be there.

All those small changes began to add up to a much larger change.

What's next? I asked myself.

After twenty-two years in Los Angeles, I moved back to New York.

Even now, as I sit here writing this book, while sipping coffee in my favorite neighborhood deli, I can't believe I did it. Almost no one moves back after an extended stay in L.A. (and even fewer attempt it at my age). But I did it.

Has it been the answer to all my problems? No. Was it the right thing for me to do? Absolutely. For reasons that I'll go into shortly.

Scary or not, sometimes we have to change our position—artistically, psychologically, or literally. To be a professional creative artist means we're in the business of exploring, understanding, and truthfully representing the many machinations of life. And as any observant person can tell you, life does not stand still.

So if the ground you've been farming is not fertile anymore, admit it. And move on. Find a new piece of ground and start tilling that soil. I'm not suggesting that means you have to pull up and move across the country like I did, but I am suggesting that if you want to stay engaged and stimulated as an artist, you may need to make a "move" of some kind, even if it's just from one way of thinking to another. Whatever kind of art you are making, it's got to come out of where you are today. If you don't like where you are, get some help and make a "move." Chances are you have little to lose, and everything to gain.

Four thoughts before we move on:

1. There is no sin in asking for or receiving help. If you need a little, get it.

2. At a certain point, the only question worth asking is "What's next?"

3. My favorite saying on this subject is "Nothing changes if nothing changes."

4. This sign hangs in my office: Stop looking. Start finding.

Show business is not for the faint-hearted. Seriously. Think about the kind of life you want to lead. Give yourself a few years in, and constantly reevaluate if you are still happy, still achieving the goals you set. If yes, continue. If not, reconsider the career. It is not a crime to leave show business!! It may be liberating.

—Nina, Broadway theatre actor and comedian

27

EXIT STRATEGY

———

When to Get Out

More than once I've sat opposite a friend and told them I was seriously considering leaving the business. However, as the old saying goes, the entertainment industry is a lot like organized crime: hard to infiltrate and virtually impossible to get out of alive.

"The business" has been good to me. Aside from a few survival jobs when I was younger, it's basically all I've ever known. In hindsight, I suspect that the entertainment gods probably laughed at my childish threats to jump ship. After all, where would I go? But twice I've come very close to leaving.

The first time was when I realized that I was only eighteen months away from my fortieth birthday. I had been in L.A. for a while, and although I'd managed to break into the screenwriting game, I hadn't scored many points. I felt a little old to be chasing a dream, but I had no real exit strategy either. I remember saying out loud to my empty apartment, "If things don't turn around before I'm forty, I'm leaving. Seriously, I am." And for the first time, I didn't feel scared uttering those words. A month later, I was asked to pitch on an adaptation of a cool (but not very cinematic) novel. I knew the project had a long history and that several writers had fallen on their swords trying to crack it. The producers were nervous and indecisive, but strangely I was not. I had a strong vision for the script, and no matter how many times they summoned me back to explain it to them (six!), I never much wavered from my original idea. For the first time in my life, I didn't care who got the assignment. I was leaving the business anyway. If they didn't hire me, it would just be one more excellent reason to get off this stupid merry-go-round.

On my thirty-ninth birthday, my agent called to say I had gotten the job. It was the first serious money I ever made in L.A.

My second attempt was a little more painful. In late 2003, fortune was smiling on the house of Bottrell. I was a fairly hot writer, and now (after a long run of "almosts") I had two very cool, very different movies in preproduction. The first was a funny and genuinely unique script that now had a big fat star attached. The second was an animated musical that everyone was hugely excited about. Unbelievably, both films were yanked out of production within thirty days of each other. Somehow the stink of that double disaster rubbed off on me, and my run of luck dissolved. I was tired of fighting windmills, and—maybe because I was in sort of a vulnerable space—I allowed myself to fall head over heels for somebody who was battling a few demons of his own. When he got a job offer in D.C., I was all too eager to abandon L.A. and join him. In the fall of 2004, we were married (in Massachusetts, where it was legal), and I then spent a curious year living in our nation's capital, while flying back to L.A. every few weeks to interview for writing jobs I didn't really want. The monthly commute began to develop into a pattern. I would fly to L.A. prepping for my meetings, then fly back to D.C. looking at college catalogues online. I knew my days in entertainment were numbered. Living in a non–show business city (with a non–show business husband) was slowly pulling me out of my dizzying orbit and back to earth where the real people lived. I was waking up to the whole concept that partnership, real estate, retirement accounts, step-kids, family, politics, religion, and worthy causes were not things you attended to when you happened to have a little extra time. This was my life now—and it was time to invest in it.

When my romance unexpectedly imploded in the summer of 2005, I found myself on a plane headed back to L.A. with no return ticket. I was broke, careerless, and in a state of complete emotional devastation. I hid in my apartment (which, thank God, I had not given up) and wondered what exactly I was going to do now. I still wanted out of the business, but I had no marketable skills outside of entertainment. I knew I should get a job of some kind, but I was paralyzed with fear.

Then one morning, while standing at my kitchen sink, I had an idea for a short film that struck me as pretty darn funny. In fact, the idea actually made me laugh out loud for the first time in weeks. Not knowing what else to do, I went up to my office, and ten hours later, I had written it. Thirty days later I shot it (on borrowed money). Ninety days later, I screened it. In the following eighteen months, it would screen at over 130 film festivals and win seventeen awards. It led to my optioning and adapting a book that would revive my sputtering screenwriting career. As a result of asking a casting director friend to help me with my "short," she thought of me when casting a freaky character role. That role would morph into the previously mentioned recurring gig on *Boston Legal*, which not only paid my bills for several months but also gave me back a wonderful, totally unexpected second career as an actor. And somehow, in the course of this frantic flurry of activity, Humpty Dumpty was put back together again.

The only good part about being shot out of a cannon is you can sometimes get an extraordinary view from up there. It gets a little easier to see that while certain roads do end, others simply fork in a new direction. I've had many friends who've happily transitioned into civilian life, but I don't think that's my fate. I realize that show business isn't a particularly noble profession, but its best products still require people with artistry, commitment, and a certain surplus of heart. I also know how easy it is to get trapped in show business limbo, where just the hope of working becomes strangely sufficient—indeed, almost preferable sometimes to the messy realities of an actual job. I still cling to the theory that wherever there is a pile of crap, there must be a pony nearby.

Yes, it's scary, but hard as I try, I can't think of another profession that would have allowed me to have as much fun as I have had in the last thirty-five years. I guess that's a little selfish. I know it's not as good as curing cancer, making a billion dollars, or having a star on the Walk of Fame, but (as my first agent used to say) "It's not exactly chopped liver either."

I have cheered loud and long for every friend of mine who has opted to exit show business. I am always genuinely happy for them. Although some have had feelings of regret, most have not. Most have breathed a huge sigh of relief.

If the idea of stepping away creates a sense of relief in you, pay attention to that instinct. It might be time to consider a new path. If you are not truly pursuing a career in the business and have not pursued one for some time, or if even the idea of pursuing one makes you feel tired, pay attention to that.

Years ago, a close friend of mine left her acting career when things were going extremely well. In her words: "One day I went to an audition for a big TV show and I realized I wasn't nervous. I got the job. A year later, I opened on Broadway, and wasn't nervous about that either. I realized I didn't care anymore.

I had gone into the business primarily because my mother told me not to. I just wanted to find out if I could do it. Once I achieved those goals, I began to think about what truly mattered to me. I wanted kids. I wanted to work at home alongside my husband. I wanted a nice house. I decided to step aside and make a little extra room for other actors who truly wanted to take the ball and run with it." And by the way, she and her husband had two kids and created a first-class PR company. I visited them at their home office many times, and they were always laughing.

Seven things to keep in mind if you are considering exiting:

1. The only reason to become a professional in the industry is if you truly love the work. Not the trappings or the glitz. The work is the only reason.

2. Without that deep, abiding love of the art form, it will be very difficult to put up with the crap.

3. If (after a reasonable time period) you don't find a niche in the industry that can provide you with enough money to live above the poverty line, you might want to consider your future.

4. I would never discourage anyone from pursuing their dream, especially a young person. But if you suspect that you are no longer in the "young" category, and you are starting to feel desperate, seriously depressed, or utterly hopeless, I'm going to suggest that you start looking at alternative dreams. There are many amazing options.

5. I was once told to "follow the love," and it was the best advice I ever got. I've shared it often. I've had friends and students who have followed their love of kids into teaching, their love of cooking into being chefs, their love of animals into veterinary school, their love of nature into careers in environmental science. There are many corners of the world that need talented, creative, brave, focused people to apply their passion to improving our human experience.

6. As I said earlier in this book, the real world is a wonderful place.

7. I have no interest in raining on anybody's parade. In fact, I wrote this book so I could cheer all of you on from the sidelines. I truly believe that the only winners in the game of life are the people who die feeling happy about how they spent their time. That is the only answer. It has always been the only answer. And it will always be the only answer. If you are happy doing whatever you are doing, *keep going!* You have my utmost admiration, respect, and complete support!

**THE BEST THING ABOUT
SHOW BUSINESS?**
The challenge it offers me. Each
new script is like a jigsaw puzzle.
All the pieces are there, and I have
to attempt to put it all together.

**THE WORST THING ABOUT
SHOW BUSINESS?**
Learning to cope with rejection.
I've had to develop a thick skin.

—Loretta, octogenarian TV and commercials character actor;
started her career at age seventy

28

JUST PAST FAMOUS

———

Late Bloomers

In 2007, I had just finished my stint on *Boston Legal* when my sister was diagnosed with advanced colon cancer. Given the hereditary factors associated with that disease, my doctor deemed it a good idea for me to have my first-ever colonoscopy. Because I know myself rather well, I opted to pay an extra $250 to be anesthetized during the procedure. I wasn't particularly worried about the discomfort factor. I just didn't like the idea of having to make small talk while someone had a camera up my ass. When I woke up, the gastroenterologist who had performed the procedure was hovering over me, gently calling my name in a warm, fatherly tone of voice. He asked me how I felt, and I groggily replied "Fine." Then, leaning in ever so slightly, he smiled and whispered in a confidential sort of way, "Did I happen to mention that I'm a big *Boston Legal* fan?"

I was genuinely shocked when I found myself on a prestigious, highly rated TV show, in a brilliantly written recurring role, at age forty-seven. It had utterly come out of the blue. The day I got the fateful call from the casting director, I had not acted (or auditioned) in over seven years. I truly had no intention of returning to acting. Then the character's ensuing popularity took me completely by surprise. I kept thinking *Now? Now, this is happening?*

I have often had actors come to my classes who are rebooting their careers. Some had a few decent credits but left because they needed to raise and support their kids. Some just lost faith early on and have always regretted not pursuing their dream. Many times, their question for me is, "Am I too late? Can I still get in the door?" My answer is, "I have no idea, but anything is possible in show business." Other times, people who have chugged along for decades, booking a job here and there, but now want to revitalize their careers, ask me, "How do I reinvent myself, so I can get the industry's attention?"

Let me repeat: anything is possible. Not guaranteed. Nor, in some cases, likely. But anything is possible.

Sometimes success is all in the timing. Often the first step is to reframe the situation. Maybe you really are just as terrific as you secretly think you are. Maybe the stars haven't quite aligned yet. No one quite understands how certain people wind up at the end of the line. Occasionally, you're so far back in the line, you forget there even is a line—especially since it doesn't seem to move very often.

When I was in acting school, I did a scene with another young actor whose work I loved. I also adored him as a person. He was a big teddy bear sort of guy, who because of his size seemed older than he was. I remember our teacher one day saying there's nothing harder than being a young character actor. I didn't know what that meant, but for the next few years my friend, although very talented, struggled to find a career. Then he passed forty, and everything changed very fast. He's since been in countless films and TV shows, and a few months ago I had the great pleasure of watching him be both hilarious and heartbreaking in a big Broadway show.

Another friend, also a character actor, achieved "hot actor" status seemingly overnight. Although she had plugged away doing very respectable supporting work for decades, it wasn't until she was in her late forties that a role came along that very quickly put her on the short list of actors who are now hard to get, because they are booked so far in advance.

When I first moved to New York, I saw Morgan Freeman in a Broadway play, and I remember thinking, Wow . . . He's so much better than he was on The Electric Company (a kids' show that aired on PBS many years ago). Then I saw him in a little off-Broadway show called Driving Miss Daisy, and the rest, as they say, is history. He was in his early fifties the first time his name appeared above the title.

There are some sobering realities to getting older in show business. The roles are less plentiful. And they get smaller. And worst of all, the competition gets considerably stiffer. Suddenly, you are going up against former "A-listers" who, having lost their leading actor status, are all too happy to play that character role you might have booked otherwise.

I know one regularly employed character actor who, when I asked him the secret to his recent success, simply shrugged and said the name of another character actor who had recently passed away. When I asked what that meant, he replied, "I had to wait for him to die."

There are legendary stories about late-blooming careers: Mae West (forty years old when she stepped off the train in Hollywood), Estelle Getty (in her sixties when she snagged her first real TV job on *The Golden Girls*), Richard Farnsworth (fifty when he received the first of his two Oscar nominations), Margo Martindale (in her sixties when she won her first Emmy), Christoph Waltz (fifty-one when he won the first of his two Oscars). Samuel L. Jackson's career-changing role was in *Pulp Fiction*, at age forty-five. Jane Lynch was forty-three when she got her big break in the mockumentary *Best in Show*. Ken Jeong was known as Dr. Ken Jeong until he was forty. Thelma Ritter was no kid at forty-eight when she started racking up Oscar nominations (six in total). I have no idea what the backstory truly is on any of these wonderful artists, other than to say I suspect they were ready when the phone rang. Truly ready. They had not lost their zeal, their enthusiasm, their willingness to return the ball over the net. I also doubt that many of them were expecting it. Success found them because they held out. Kept the torch lit. Not for fame, but for the sheer joy of doing their art.

If you are an established actor wanting to revive your career, or someone who is entering the business at a later age, I will tell you it can be a little complex. Mostly because of the seasoned competition you will face. Is it possible to break in? Yes, it is. It will largely depend on your talent and your willingness to work harder than anyone around you. It will be humbling at times. And more difficult than you'd like it to be. And it will also depend on your love of the art form. But it is possible.

If you are hoping for major fame, that will be trickier.

About a decade ago, it occurred to me that I'm never going to be famous. At least not in that "major artist" kind of way. I'll have my moments here and there (like occasional recognition from medical personnel), but I'm not going to win an Oscar or sit in a box at the Kennedy Center Honors. Don't get me wrong. It's not like the industry has ignored me. Quite the opposite. In fact, it's been pretty generous to me. When I was younger, I was so driven and focused and insufferably determined to "be somebody." I wish I had realized at the time that I already was somebody, and that fame, when you boil it down, is just a light someone shines on you. It can only illuminate who you already are and can sometimes blind you to what ultimately matters. Had I known that thirty years ago, I might have taken things a little easier and hit fewer walls.

The revelation that Godot is not coming has been strangely freeing. The last few years have been, hands down, the most fun and artistically satisfying of my whole career. The decision to allow the tide to steer the boat has paid some glorious dividends in both the writing and the acting camps. It's odd to realize that my fantasies gave me a life, and now life is giving me back those fantasies. As my hero, Mark Twain, once said, "Fame is a vapor; popularity an accident; the only earthly certainty is oblivion." Maybe not the cheeriest way of putting it, but I don't disagree. A long time ago, I was fortunate enough to be let into a club that celebrates dreaming and dreamers, and I'll gladly perform in their talent show as long as they'll have me.

Seven thoughts about starting (or blooming) late:

1. Anything is possible. That's one of the things I love most about show business.

2. That said, we all need to look at the odds and make informed decisions that we can live with.

3. Starting later means you are a more mature person. That's not a bad thing. You know more about life and are probably more courageous about sharing that knowledge through your work. As an artist you'll have more to offer.

4. Lots of professional actors reach a certain age and (for all intents and purposes) cease to pursue the work. They might keep their union dues paid up (just in case), but they no longer have any real interest in the hustling needed to land the next gig. So, on the one hand, if you are entering later in the game, the competition decreases as you go along.

5. On the flip side, the number of roles for older actors also decreases, so your competition from those still in the running gets stiffer. A few years ago I went in to audition for a fairly mundane character role on a TV show. When I signed in with the receptionist, I was floored to see the names of two very well-known (aka famous) actors who had already auditioned for this role earlier in the day. One of them had a Tony! Ironically, none of us got the role. When I later looked online to see who did book it, I discovered the actor had very few credits. So, like I said: anything is possible.

6. Older actors can often find great opportunities in the independent film world. New filmmakers don't often have access to (or the budget to pay) established actors. If you wind up in such a film and it goes to a festival, try to attend the screenings. That's always a great way to meet other new filmmakers who might want to hire you.

7. Late bloomers can also find opportunities working in TV commercials. Many commercial agents are very open to actors who do not have an extensive resume. Although it's usually not artistically fulfilling work, it can gain you entry into the union, earn you a little money, and put your face out there. Note: You can easily find lists of commercial agents online on websites like Backstage.com.

I'm a prime case in that you can be anything you want to be. I'm a hyphenate. I'm an actor-writer-producer-director and sometimes casting director. Casting pays my bills. I still get to act every single day in the room with other actors. And when I go home, I write scripts. I produce theatre that *I can do*. Never let anyone tell you who you can or cannot be. If they say "You can't be that," smile, flip them off, and say "Watch me."

—Tyler, actor, writer, producer, director, and casting director, formerly based in L.A., now based in Savannah and Atlanta

29

BORDER CROSSINGS

———

The New Frontier

I have an acquaintance who lives in Austin, Texas, and regularly books jobs in TV and film. Although she's done a lot of work, she's not what you'd call famous. She's just very, very good. She got tired of living in L.A. and told her agents she was moving to Austin. They squawked a little, but it all worked out.

Another actor-friend I've known since we were waiters together in New York now lives in New Orleans with his wife and kids. He still has the same agent, self-tapes his auditions, books work all the time, and has traveled all over making movies. It worked out.

I have a friend who tried New York for a year and hated it. He moved to Chicago, where he has lived ever since. He's represented locally and has had a great career in theatre, commercials, and voice-over work. It worked out.

Another friend moved back to Nashville to take care of an aging parent. She found local representation and suddenly began to book much larger and better roles in many of the projects that now regularly shoot in the Southeast. These gigs included a very big recurring role on a network show. The same was true for two students of mine who moved to Atlanta. They're working more there. Another friend of mine moved to Florida twenty years ago and has stayed consistently employed in theatre (and met his amazing wife there). In all cases, it worked out.

It's a new day. The structure of our industry is shifting almost hourly. The way entertainment is created, produced, shot, and distributed is undergoing a giant sea change. Some of it is wonderful. Some of it is terrifying. In many ways it feels like the Wild West out there. But the great thing about the Wild West was that it was a frontier. And on any frontier, there are always lots and lots of opportunities for prospectors, homesteaders, outlaws, and visionaries.

I'd venture to say that even as you are reading this, something new is being developed or introduced. Some new model is being road-tested. With the incredible jumps technology keeps taking, God knows where our industry is headed next.

I offer this to you because I think it's an exciting time to be in the entertainment business, because these rule-breakers, innovators, and (my favorite new job description) content providers are becoming the new saviors of the industry. In my experience, whenever one watering hole goes dry in our business, another is suddenly discovered, and the herd stampedes in that direction. This has always been true and always will be. The longer I'm in entertainment, the more faith I have that it will probably last forever. The human race needs us to distract, nudge, and inspire them. Probably now more than ever.

If you are being kept busy by the industry, that's fantastic! Congratulations! Enjoy it and find ways to make that steady stream of jobs serve your greater long-term goals.

If, however, you are not overwhelmed with opportunities, perhaps you should consider where all that great creative energy of yours could (or should) be going. If you are being called to create something of your own, perhaps you should find a way to do it. If there was ever a time to try something new, it's now. I think Teddy Roosevelt got it right when he (supposedly) said, "Do what you can, with what you have, wherever you are."

Perhaps your inner voice is screaming, *I can't. I don't know how. I don't know where to start. It's impossible.* My answer is, "You're right. It is impossible. It has always been impossible. It will always be impossible. But oddly, that never stops people from creating something new." Someone started something new today. Someone will start something new tomorrow. As I've mentioned, I woke up one morning in 2013 with an idea about starting a science fiction one-act play festival. The idea was so exciting, but I had almost no experience as a theatre producer. *This is crazy,* I told myself. *It's overwhelming! It'll cost a fortune!* (All of which were true.) But the idea wouldn't go away. So I finally took a deep breath and picked up my phone. One year later, our first festival opened to sold-out houses and phenomenal reviews. So forget the impossible part and go ahead and do it anyway. If you don't know how to do something, just start making calls until you find someone who can tell you how to do it or loves doing that thing. Maybe they'll love that thing so much, they'll do it for you. If you are by nature more of a team player than a trailblazer, then find someone who is a leader by nature (preferably someone insanely talented) and offer them your full support. Become part of their crew. Join their cheering section. It's important.

We are living in a time when the rules that clearly defined what was possible and what was not seem to be disappearing. That doesn't mean that things won't continue to be tough and confusing from time to time. When I set out to write this book, I was hoping to offer you some answers, but then I remembered about halfway through that *there aren't any*. There are only new questions to be wrestled with. New puzzles to solve. New cliffs to be jumped off of. New deals to be struck. New borders to be crossed.

Once upon a time, actors toured the country in wagons putting on shows for donations (and the occasional sack of potatoes). They wrote new plays and did Shakespeare (sometimes rewriting the endings so characters like Hamlet and Romeo and Juliet didn't die in the end). This usually resulted in more potatoes and sometimes a chicken. In short, they bent the old rules. They continually adapted to circumstances. They entertained. They created something a little different every day. Not a bad policy in the world we currently live in.

The industry has become more corporate, which is sad, because it means many of the largest and most lucrative projects are now forced to take their marching orders from the marketing department. As projects grow more expensive, our employers want to minimize risk. Ideas get homogenized, and the goal is to force the project to appeal to the largest demographic possible. While this is a little depressing, it also requires all of us to be a little more creative and find new ways to get our worthwhile ideas into the marketplace. This will be our challenge for the foreseeable future, so the sooner we all step up and find solutions, the better.

I can assure you of one thing: you have more power than you think you do. So if the existing rules don't fit you, write some new ones that will. Find your voice as an artist. Then find a way to use it. Then find an audience for it. The size of that audience doesn't matter. Just do it. Assume that the world needs your art until you're told otherwise. In fact, even *after* being told otherwise, do your thing anyway. Only *you* can bring forth what's already alive inside your imagination and heart.

So get started. We're all waiting for you.

Five thoughts about the new realities of the business:

1. Careers used to exclusively start in either New York or L.A. Now careers can start in places like Atlanta (where there's a lot of production at the moment). Sometimes starting in a smaller market is a good way to build your resume before moving to a bigger market.

2. On the flip side, some established performers are moving to smaller markets because they've grown tired of living in large expensive cities like New York and L.A.

3. A few years ago, putting a lot of time and money into self-producing an internet web series seemed like a huge waste of time. Now those series (when beautifully written and produced) are being bought by companies like Netflix, and their creators are selling new ideas to networks. Provided the work is good, it's a new day.

4. When I was a young actor, I thought that acting was all I would ever do. In fact, I couldn't bear the idea of doing anything else. Now, if I thought all I would ever do in my career is act, I'd probably retire. Don't get me wrong, I still love it, but I've also had enormous fun working as a writer, director, and producer. These jobs cause me to use a different part of my brain and require some very advanced people skills—and wow, there's quite a bit of joy that can come with creating, shaping, or guiding a new project into existence. Try it!

5. There was a time when switching sides of the aisle (actor to writer, writer to director, director to actor) carried a big stigma. The conventional wisdom was that you'd abandoned one camp for another and would never be returning. That's no longer really the case. Yes, the industry loves to pigeonhole people because it's easier. That will never change. Be smarter than they are. Do what you need to do. Here's my biggest piece of advice to you: don't let your path be wholly determined by what the industry is buying today. Next month they will want something else. Don't ask the industry what they'd like you to be. Become who you are. And when you outgrow that persona, become something else. The industry needs *you*. Let the industry find you for one simple reason: because you are too good not to be found.

**THE BEST THING ABOUT
SHOW BUSINESS?**
Per diem and craft service.

**THE WORST THING ABOUT
SHOW BUSINESS?**
Memorizing lines.

—Gavin, leading man and series regular on iconic TV show

30

BURNING QUESTIONS

———

FAQs from the Freshly Launched

Because I wanted to make sure I'd covered my bases, I sent out an email to ten of my former students, all of whom are recent graduates from the colleges, studios, and conservatories where I sometimes teach. I asked them all to give me five questions they hoped a book like this might answer. Needless to say, a wide variety of topics came up, but there was also a lot of common ground. Here are the five questions most frequently asked and what I hope are some helpful answers.

How do I keep in contact with important people in a non-annoying way?

At this stage of your career, I'd say your important people probably fall into two categories: (a) friends and acquaintances who are starting to work in the business, and (b) professional contacts like agents, managers, and casting directors. In the case of friends who are experiencing some success, I'd say the best plan is to congratulate them every time you hear that something good has happened in their lives or careers. Everybody in this industry works hard, and it's nice to be acknowledged for your work. If you do this, chances are when they hear that *you're* doing something, it will be more likely to show up on their radar, and they might become a valuable ally in the future. When it comes to agents, managers, and casting directors, they are very used to people "staying in touch." Be someone who actually has some news to share. Let them know when you are doing a play, a student film, or anything else! Generally speaking, they tend to be more interested in busy people.

If you want to produce something—a play or an independent film—how do you fund it?

For theatre, if you want to do something out of the Samuel French play catalog, you'll have to pay royalties for the use of that script. Shakespeare is free, as are the works of a few other long-dead writers. For everything else (including adaptations), check the rights before you announce it to the world. Theatre costs money, so pass the hat and produce it as cheaply as possible (which doesn't necessarily mean in a traditional theatre space). Regarding your budget: Keep in mind that usually only people you personally know will contribute to your crowd-funding campaign. Strangers rarely do. If you want to do a new play (or have written one), the best plan is to start with a few public readings, which can happen in any large space that has some folding chairs. That process will allow you to gradually refine both the script and a game plan for how to produce it. If the script is good, you'll be surprised how many people will be willing to help you. If you want to do an indie film, I'd suggest doing a short film first. It's much cheaper and will teach you a lot about filmmaking. If the short looks good, it will help you enlist the support of more people who could help shepherd a feature-length project to the finish line. Believe it or not, those people will come from simply asking around. In show business, even in the early stages, everybody knows somebody. Just keep asking.

How do I deal with the rejections, anxiety, nerves, and depression that come along with trying to break into the business?

The term "breaking in" is meant to serve as a warning that there is rarely a red carpet rolled out for newcomers. The early years of anyone's career are going to be a little tough at times. Most of those creepy feelings are a result of feeling frightened that you aren't "good enough" to ever get paid for your work. That's understandable, but only time will tell. Give the "breaking in" process three solid years of your life and see how you feel about it then. Those fears tend to lessen as your confidence in your skills increases. But keep in mind, skills and confidence increase only if you are practicing your art. So practice like crazy for those three years. In the meantime, release all those rejections, anxiety, and depression into the ether by remembering that every famous actor you admire has felt them as well. These feelings are a rite of passage. Move through them and on to the next stage of your journey.

How do you find audition monologues that are right for you? And how do you create a reel with no major TV/film credits to put on it?

At the beginning of your career, agents and casting directors often will want you to have a monologue or two ready to go at a moment's notice. These monologues need to be a perfect fit for the actor who is performing them. Think of it like shopping for a piece of clothing you'd want to wear to a very important party. It needs to be flattering and age-appropriate and should reflect your personality. You want it to feel fresh and hip—something that will get you a little attention. All of these are great things to think about when choosing material for yourself. Don't do something that's more appropriate for your grandmother than for you. Don't do something that is miles away from the sort of characters you are ready to play *today*. You should love performing this monologue, and you should have more than one. How do you find them? By constantly looking for them and asking other actors where they have found theirs. Be careful about performing monologues that contain extremely vulgar language or very explicit sexual content. Your monologues are usually used to introduce yourself as an actor and are sometimes performed in relatively small office spaces. Just be aware that you don't know these people you're auditioning for (or their history), so extreme in-your-face material could wind up offending them. In regard to reels, I suggest you go online and look at early auditions done by actors who are now very famous. Those pieces of film are very short but show an actor connected and in the moment. If you don't have any TV and film credits, write yourself a short little two-person scene (or ask a friend to help you) and shoot it with your phone (or a decent camera if you can borrow one). When I say short, I mean short. Like one minute long. Take a little time to plan out things like your lighting and location. Make it look and sound as good as you can, and do multiple takes until you get a version you love! Then edit it and post it online. Use that as your reel until you have something professional to replace it. If you can act, I promise you it'll be clear in that very short scene. If you are not confident in your camera skills, take a class and practice. Don't waste your time and money until you're sure you can deliver.

With all of the uncertainty, how do you plan your life?

Every human being on the planet attempts to plan their life in one way or another, and in many, many cases it's life that winds up calling the shots. That's not to say we can't make a few decisions based on what we genuinely care about and what we'd like to have happen in the future. I recommend that you begin with a general game plan and try to stay fluid, while keeping an eye on your savings account. If, for instance, you know that in the long run you want kids, begin to adjust your priorities accordingly, so that having a family life can eventually become a happy reality. If you want to buy a house, start figuring out when and where you want that to happen. I always knew I wanted to start in theatre in New York. It was my first love, even though I knew I'd never make much money doing it. I also always knew I wanted to try my hand at TV and film in L.A. My first attempt at L.A. was a disaster because I wasn't remotely ready for such a huge sea change either artistically or personally. When I came back the next time, I had a much clearer view of my goals and much more realistic expectations. I understood the business better, and as a result, I made a little money. I knew I wanted to return to New York at some point, and eventually I did (although it took a lot longer than I thought it would). The beauty of the work we do is that when it's done well, it's a wonderfully true reflection of human life. One of our primary jobs as artists is to stay present in our own lives, so we can sense when the wind is changing direction. Trust your instincts. They are rarely wrong.

I've been asked many times, "How do I 'make it' in this business?" I'm never sure how to answer that, but a few key points do stand out. So . . .

Here are seven things that genuinely matter for "making it":

1. You must truly believe that you already have everything you need. All you have to do is grow and deepen those things.

2. The complaint I hear most frequently from industry professionals about meetings with young performers is that the newbies largely seem intimidated and unable to answer the simplest questions, like: What kind of characters do you like to play? What kind of shows do you like? Keep in mind that it's very hard to help people who can't enjoy a little harmless creative conversation in what is a widely creative business. If this is true of you, fix it. Make this journey fun.

3. Lots of people like to talk about the need for discipline. I'm here to tell you discipline is a dry, unappealing concept that will not take you far in this business. What *will* get you out of bed in the morning to pursue your dreams is *enthusiasm*. Not just for your personal dreams but for the art form you are pursuing. Find out everything you can about your craft. Fall in love with all of it. Everything. And keep that love burning and alive.

4. If you are lucky enough to be visited by success early in your career, don't for a second assume it's your birthright or that it will last forever. Every truly successful artist I know who was blessed with early entry began to strategize (while the grass was still green) as to where they might land next.

5. Be respectful of everybody. Always. That includes set, costume, and lighting designers, hair and makeup people, crew members, assistants, security guards, and unpaid interns. Their work is as important as yours.

6. Say "thank you" as often as possible. Although it may sometimes feel like you're doing this all by yourself, you're not. Over the course of your career, many others will be involved. Do not forget to thank them for their efforts on your behalf. It matters.

7. Although it will sometimes appear that everyone else has all the answers, they don't. Believe it or not, people who win the Oscar wake up the next morning and wonder where their career will go next. The whole thing is a journey with no guaranteed destination. As I said before, everybody's path is completely unique. If you're going to do this, don't be scared of that fact. Embrace it. Explore it. And enjoy all the cool stuff it offers.

AFTERWORD

———

Is It All Worth It?

By early 2009, I'd already had my little taste of fame from *Boston Legal*. It had been fun at first, but after a couple of years of being tapped on the shoulder by fans at the dry cleaners, at the airport, or in the middle of lunch with a friend, it was getting old. There are only so many times you can enjoy being asked, "What's James Spader [or William Shatner or Candice Bergen or Julie Bowen] really like?" All you can say is, "They're great." The real answer probably should have been, "I have no idea. They're probably just human beings like the rest of us, but honestly, I don't really know. We just shot a few scenes together. We didn't really hang out or anything."

Don't get me wrong. I don't mean to suggest that I didn't genuinely like my coworkers (I did!) or wasn't grateful and flattered that so many people stopped me to say they had appreciated my work. But turning to find an expectant stranger with a burning question about Lincoln Meyer was not as much fun as it had been two years earlier.

So when I turned around in Ralph's Supermarket on Sunset Boulevard that morning in 2009 to find an attractive sixtyish woman squinting suspiciously at me, I braced myself.

"Are you an actor?" she asked, somewhat pointedly.

"Yes, I am."

"I know you from somewhere . . ."

This wasn't the first time I'd encountered this form of "I know you from" confusion, so I tried to be helpful.

"Have you ever seen *Boston Legal*?" I offered.

"No, I've never seen that show. What else have you been on?" Her tone suggested that I was trying to trick her or something.

"*Ugly Betty*?" I offered.

"No."

"*Criminal Minds?*"

"I hate that show."

"*Castle?*"

"Nope."

"*iCarly?*"

"Never seen it."

"Okay, I'm sorry," I finally said, fearing that the frozen chicken I was holding was going to defrost before we found the answer. "I've been in a lot of stuff."

"Were you in *A Midsummer Night's Dream* in Buffalo, New York, in 1985?"

I almost dropped my chicken. "Yes—I was," I stammered, utterly amazed.

"And you were the guy who was in the play, the one they performed for the king! And you had to wear a dress because your character was supposed to be playing some kinda princess, right?"

"Yes, that's right."

"And the dress was way too tight, and you couldn't sit down, but you kept trying to, for like a minute, right?" she said, her excitement rising.

Her memory was spot-on. The dress bit was something I had suggested to the costumer, who had constructed a gown for me that was basically impossible to sit down in. Every night I worked that gag for a least a minute or longer, carefully wringing out the single longest continuous laugh I've ever gotten out of an audience. It was utterly shameless, and also one of the most fun things I've ever done in my entire career.

"I'm amazed you remember that!"

Her face became strangely serious. "I can't tell you how many times over the last twenty-five years I have laughed myself to sleep thinking about that moment."

I shook her hand and thanked her for her very kind words.

What I didn't tell her was that that exchange in the frozen food aisle was the single most profound moment I have to date experienced as an artist.

A lot of us go through our careers wondering if what we do matters. And to whom? And on what level does it matter? Is it just something we do because it feels good? Do we do it for love? Attention? To amuse ourselves? Are we striving for some sense of immortality? And what is the purpose of all this insanity anyway?

It's taken me a while to define what it is I "do" in this business (and why), but here is what I have come up with: I think I am in the mental health field.

I believe artists are the teachers and mediums of the world. We reflect life back to our audience, so that they can see what it looks like to take a stand, to fight the good fight, to survive a terrible turn of events, to lose gracefully, to surrender control, to hang onto what is worthy, to recognize what ultimately matters, or to laugh fully and deeply at the absurdity of our all-too-brief existence.

That conversation in the frozen food section of Ralph's was a great, great reminder of why our work is important.

If we do our job well, it doesn't really matter where we do it. It doesn't matter if we do it on screen with ten million people watching or in a church basement with four people in attendance. If we bring a little truth into the room, if we're courageous, if we give our whole selves to the task and successfully pull off the tale we are telling, *someone in that audience will remember it until the day they die.* And that is what makes it worth all the effort. That is what makes it beautiful. That is what makes it art.

Most days I think I'm pretty good at what I do, but I'm not brilliant. I have been successful by my own personal definition of that word, and I have tried hard to never measure my success by fame or huge sums of money. I've measured it in laughter. My own, and the laughter I've been able to offer to others: my coworkers, my friends, and, of course, any audience who was willing to watch.

There have been times in the last six months that I've asked myself, *Who the hell are you to be writing this book?* And the answer has always been, *Who am I not to write this book?*

I don't really think I chose this life. I think it chose me. And I am as happy to feel "chosen" today as I was when I was a very young man on a bus headed for New York City. I am and will always be grateful.

If this is your path, you will know it. I am very happy to pass you the torch with the sincere hope that you will laugh as much during your career as I have laughed during mine—which is not really a career at all.

It's a life.

And there is no life quite like it.

Welcome to show business. If *you* believe in you, then I believe in you. Now go out there and knock 'em dead.

I ASKED MY VERY TALENTED AND SMART FRIENDS: WHAT'S THE BEST PIECE OF ADVICE YOU CAN OFFER TO THE READERS OF THIS BOOK?

Work hard. Be kind. And never give up. If you give up, it'll never get better.

—Victoria, TV writer, series creator, and showrunner

It's a numbers game. Go on every audition you can, and treat auditioning as a job. Getting in the door is half the struggle, and every time you audition it just ups your percentage of getting the next job.

—Imani, indie TV and film actor and producer

Try not to think negatively on why you would be wrong for a project. Think, *What have I to offer?* A career as an actor or performer or any creative artist is a journey toward self-knowledge and a continual search for self-definition. What do you have to offer?

—Laurence, iconic New York theatre performer and playwright

There's never one "right" way to do anything.

—Danielle, film and television producer and network executive

The head of casting of CBS saw me in a small off-Broadway show and called me in for a meeting. He told me I was very talented, so he wanted to pass on some advice. "Learn to wait *creatively*. And the people who are truly important in this business never act like it."

—Roz, popular theatre, TV, and film actor

Don't leave your accounting job if you have one.

—Mike, actor and writer (and former accountant)

Know your lines, let the stunt people do the stunts, and don't be an asshole.

—Gavin, leading man and series regular on iconic TV show

While most of us want to be the next Meryl Streep, you can always expand your skill set by studying comedy; if you are only seen as a "serious" actor, then you cut yourself out of half the work in New York or Hollywood. You can take classes at Second City or UCB that can absolutely hone that skill set.

—Carter, TV actor and series regular on hugely popular show

It's difficult. Don't have expectations. Do it because you love it, not because you want to be famous. If it is your passion, never give up.

—Charlie, leading man on cult hit TV show

Never stop studying.

—Aaron, TV and theatre director

Save your money!

—Jessica, TV and indie film producer

You are more than enough.

—Sarah, up-and-coming young actor and recent drama school grad

The trick is that you should not invest time convincing others that you are talented. Let your talent exemplify who you are, and you will attract people who appreciate you and want to work with you. Also, be humble, because you should always be listening and learning shit.

—Xavier, actor, playwright, and screenwriter

Be persistent and stay spiritually centered. Do the work for the love of the work. In the end that's really all there is.

—Frank, veteran character actor

Don't do it if you can be happy doing *anything* else.

—Lisa, off-Broadway composer

Dear readers: Never ever assume that people who are supposedly working on your behalf are actually doing their jobs. Or to put it another way: Paranoia is healthy.

—Austin, playwright and comedy writer

Don't forget to live your life. And you have permission to always say no or change your mind.

—Santiago, TV actor and voice-over artist

Listen.

—Rebecca, independent film director

Make sure you have another source of income.

—Helen, veteran TV comedy actor

There is no shame in starting at the bottom. No one cares about that. Pay attention. Stay focused. Be on time. Be prepared. *Work hard!* And remember, everyone is replaceable—you, me, even big famous people.

—Catherine, veteran TV casting director

Write a lot. Creating gives you power in this town. If you have scripts, people come to you; you have something to offer, and that makes you different than 90 percent of the town, which just has their hand out.

—Stephen, TV and film writer and producer

Stop waiting to be asked and stop asking for permission. Whenever I thought I wasn't getting what I needed (creatively), I went and created it myself. I'm one of those "I dare you to tell me no, or that's not possible" kind of people, because I'll just say "Watch me!"

—Ernie, actor and comedian

When you think you've run out of steam and can't press on, dig a little deeper and you'll find you have more to give.

—Jeremy, character actor

RESULTS

Programs and Classes

New York

THREE- TO FOUR-YEAR CONSERVATORY/DEGREE PROGRAMS

Full-time programs that cover pretty much all the bases.

The Juilliard School
www.juilliard.edu
Widely regarded as one of the world's best performing arts schools.

NYU Tisch School of the Arts
tisch.nyu.edu
Tisch had more alumni working on Broadway in 2017 than any other
school for theatre in the country.

Yale School of Drama
www.drama.yale.edu
Located in New Haven, Connecticut, approximately two and a half hours
from New York, the school operates in a unique partnership with the
Yale Repertory Theatre and is considered one of the nation's best theatre
conservatories.

The Actors Studio at Pace University
www.performingarts.pace.edu
Sanctioned by the legendary Actors Studio, the school is home to the
popular TV interview series *Inside the Actors Studio*.

TWO-YEAR CONSERVATORIES

Although usually accredited (so credits often transfer), they do not give degrees. Policies and accreditation status can change, so if that matters to you, make sure you ask.

American Musical and Dramatic Academy
www.amda.edu
Primarily known as a musical theatre school. There is also an L.A. campus.

The American Academy of Dramatic Arts
www.aada.edu
Founded in 1884, AADA is the longest continuously operating acting school in the United States. Also has an L.A. campus.

Circle in the Square Theatre School
www.circlesquare.org
The only accredited conservatory program directly associated with a Broadway theatre.

ACTING STUDIOS

Some have two-year programs, while others offer less-structured ongoing classes, allowing students to progress at their own pace. Most are associated with the methodology of a particular teacher.

William Esper Studio
www.esperstudio.com

The Barrow Group School
www.barrowgroup.org

Tom Todoroff Studio
www.tomtodoroff.com

The Maggie Flanigan Studio
www.maggieflaniganstudio.com

Ted Bardy Studio
www.tedbardy.com

The Acting Studio
www.actingstudio.com

Kelly Kimball/Kimball Studio

www.kimballstudio.com

Atlantic Acting School

www.atlanticactingschool.org/Programs

Actors Connection

www.actorsconnection.com

Not specifically a school, this organization specializes in offering seminars, workshops, and short-term classes. It's a good starting place for the beginning actor.

ICONIC ACTING SCHOOLS

These schools are usually closely aligned with the techniques created by the highly influential teachers who founded them in the 1940s, '50s, and '60s.

Neighborhood Playhouse

www.neighborhoodplayhouse.org

Teaching the methodology of Sanford Meisner. ·

HB Studio

www.hbstudio.org

Teaching the methodology of Uta Hagen and Herbert Berghof. This studio is a good fit for students on a tight budget and for those who are looking for their first-ever acting class.

Lee Strasberg Theatre & Film Institute

www.methodactingstrasberg.com

Strasberg was also one of the founders of the Actors Studio (www.theactorsstudio.org). Both organizations also have an L.A. campus.

Stella Adler Studio of Acting

www.stellaadler.com

Also has a studio in L.A.

IMPROV AND SKETCH COMEDY

If you're funny, it wouldn't hurt to at least take one class at an established improv or sketch school. It looks good on your resume and can open doors.

Upright Citizens Brigade
www.newyork.ucbtrainingcenter.com
Improv and sketch comedy school with prestigious alumni, also has an L.A. studio.

The PIT (People's Improv Theatre)
www.thepit-nyc.com
Award-winning training center with up-and-coming alumni.

Los Angeles

THREE- TO FOUR-YEAR CONSERVATORY/DEGREE PROGRAMS

Although, like New York schools, West Coast schools also offer world-class training, be aware that their aesthetic (or "vibe") is slightly different, reflecting not just the differences in geography, weather, and culture but also their proximity to the epicenter of the TV, film, and music businesses.

USC School of Dramatic Arts
www.dramaticarts.usc.edu
USC is also home to the prestigious USC film school.

UCLA School of Theater, Film and Television
www.tft.ucla.edu
For postgraduate work, also check out "Acting for the Camera" at www.professionalprograms.tft.ucla.edu.

American Conservatory Theater MFA Program
www.act-sf.org/home/conservatory/mfa_program.html
Located in San Francisco (approximately six hours north of L.A.), this program is closely associated with the prestigious American Conservatory Theater.

TWO-YEAR CONSERVATORIES

Although usually accredited (so credits often transfer), they do not give degrees. Policies and accreditation status can change, so if that matters to you, make sure you ask.

American Musical and Dramatic Academy
www.amda.edu
Primarily known as a musical theatre school. Also has a New York campus.

The American Academy of Dramatic Arts
www.aada.edu
Founded in 1884, AADA is the longest continuously operating acting school in the United States. Also has a New York campus.

ACTING STUDIOS

The majority of L.A. acting studios are firmly anchored in the techniques taught by the namesake instructor. Many of these studios divide their classes into beginner, intermediate, and advanced levels of training; others offer more of a workshop atmosphere, allowing actors of varying levels of experience to work together in the same class. Be sure to audit and ask questions before signing up.

Ivana Chubbuck
www.ivanachubbuck.com

Larry Moss
www.larrymoss.org

Howard Fine
www.howardfine.com

Lesly Kahn
www.leslykahn.com

Jeffrey Marcus
www.jeffreymarcus.com

Michelle Danner
www.michelledanner.com

Warner Loughlin
www.warnerloughlin.com

Diana Castle
www.theimaginedlife.com

Stephen Book
www.stephenbook.com

IMPROV AND SKETCH COMEDY

When it comes to comedy, even a little improv and sketch training from an established school can definitely open doors in L.A.

The Groundlings
www.groundlings.com
Tiered training program. Long list of prestigious alumni.

Upright Citizens Brigade
www.losangeles.ucbtrainingcenter.com
Also has a New York studio.

Second City
www.secondcity.com
Also has studios in Chicago and Toronto.

ACKNOWLEDGMENTS

———

Jules Aaron

Phil Abrams

Actors Equity Association

American Academy of Dramatic Arts

Avalon Artists Agency

Backstage.com

Rochelle Bates

Dudley Beene

Michael Blaha

Shauna Bloom

Joel Brady

BRS/Gage, New York and Los Angeles

Carlease Burke

Jason Buzas

Caroline and Jamie (the best neighbors in the world)

Erin Cherry

Lee Costello

Roy Cruz and the entire cast of *Streep Tease*

Robertson Dean

Bill D'Elia

Tina D'Marco

Dramatists Play Service

Barbara Dreyfus

William Esper

Everyone at Sci-Fest L.A.

Every student in every class I ever taught

Jim Fall

Don Fenner

Consuelo Flores

Laurie Fox

David Frank

Patty and Andrew Freedman

Seth Front

Katherine Fugate

Neil Gaiman

David Gillis

Brian Glass

Mark Glick

Gary Goldstein

Libby Goldstein

Ashley Green

Xaque Gruber

Charlotte Gusay

Dino Hainline

William Healey

Neil Hemnarine

Stephen McKinley Henderson

Hollywood United Methodist Church

Karen Hutson

Bill Johnson

Jessie K. Jones

Jon Jory

Steve Kaplan

Jason Kaufman

Jack Kenny

Charles D. King

Adam Lazarus

Kathy Cooper Ledesma

John Levey

Long Wharf Theatre

Warren Lyons

Elizabeth Mann

Thomas Mann

Jeffrey Marcus

Metrosource magazine

Ray McKinnon

Monnae Michaell

John Miranda

Taylor Negron

Michael Offer

Judy Orbach

Kevin Pawlowski

Peoples Light and Theatre Company

Pauley Perrette

Bil Pfuderer

John Pollono

Matthew Porter

Kemp Powers

Professional Acting School at UCLA

Alex Rapport

Mark Redanty

Matt Reidy

Jordan Roberts

Donna Rosenstein

Maggie Rowe

Ruth, Dean, Mary, and Jerry

SAG-AFTRA

Sarabeth Schedeen

Richard Schiff

Second Stage

David Shaul

Victoria Shaw

Geoffrey Sherman

Sit 'N' Spin Family

Leigh Kilton Smith

Mary Steinborn

Studio Arena Theatre

Neeley Swanson

Daniel Swee

Those two entitled shitheads who sublet my apartment

Tuesdays at Nine

Terri Wagener

Valryn Warren

Zoe Watkins

Garland Whitt

Christopher Wright

Writers Guild of America

Ronnie Yeskel

Graham Yost

And the whole team at Ten Speed Press:

Lisa Westmoreland (executive editor)

Kristi Hein (copyeditor)

Michelle Li (designer)

Eleanor Thacher (marketing and publicity)

Dan Myers (production)

ABOUT THE AUTHOR

David Dean Bottrell has been a professional actor and writer for over thirty-five years. Known for his quirky characterizations, he's played a great many guest star and recurring roles on such shows as *Modern Family*, *NCIS*, *Mad Men*, *Justified*, *True Blood*, *Longmire*, *Rectify*, *CSI*, *Bones*, *Castle*, *Criminal Minds*, *Days of Our Lives*, *iCarly*, and *Boston Legal*, to name just a few. His many theatre credits include shows at the Public Theatre, Second Stage, the Long Wharf Theatre, and Actors Theatre of Louisville's Humana Festival. He cowrote the off-Broadway play *Dearly Departed* (published by Dramatist Play Service) as well the hit film adaptation, *Kingdom Come*. Additionally, he's written screenplays for many major studios, including Disney Feature Animation, Paramount, MTV Films, and Fox Searchlight. He's taught camera acting for the UCLA Professional School, Temple University, and the American Academy of Dramatic Arts (both the New York and L.A. campuses). Over the course of his career, David has had the pleasure of working with many acclaimed writers, directors, and actors, including Angela Bassett, Kathy Bates, Candice Bergen, Craig Bierko, Julie Bowen, Delta Burke, Thomas Gibson, Whoopi Goldberg, Angie Harmon, Mark Harmon, John Heard, Anne Heche, Stephen McKinley Henderson, LL Cool J, David E. Kelley, Ian McKellen, Matthew Modine, Timothy Olyphant, Dolly Parton, Richard Schiff, James Spader, William Shatner, Matthew Weiner, and Julie White. In addition to being an accomplished spoken word artist, he occasionally writes professional advice columns for Backstage.com. Originally from Kentucky, he currently divides his time between New York and Los Angeles. For more info and to watch video clips of his work, visit DavidDeanBottrell.net.

INDEX